God

WHAT EVERY CATHOLIC SHOULD KNOW

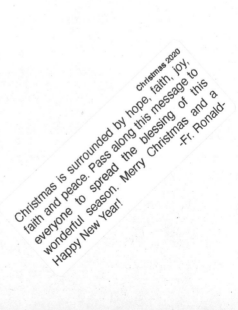

Christmas 2020

Christmas is surrounded by hope, faith, joy, faith and peace. Pass along this message to everyone to spread the blessing of this wonderful season. Merry Christmas and a Happy New Year!

-Fr. Ronald-

God

WHAT EVERY CATHOLIC SHOULD KNOW

Elizabeth Klein

IGNATIUS PRESS
San Francisco

AUGUSTINE INSTITUTE
Greenwood Village, CO

Cover art: *Christ Pantocrator*
by Fr. Justinian

Cover Design: Lisa Patterson

©2019 Ignatius Press, San Francisco,
and the Augustine Institute, Greenwood Village, CO
All rights reserved
ISBN 978-1-7338598-8-2 (pbk)
ISBN 978-1-950939-01-5 (hbk)
Library of Congress Control Number 2019941608

Printed in Canada ∞

Contents

1

We Should Desire to Know God

Given the title of this book, you may be wondering why it is so short. How could there be a shortcut or quick guide for knowing about God? Isn't the Christian life about coming to know God more and more? It is true that we can never know everything about God, and that we as Christians are always seeking to know God better. This book, however, has a specific focus: in it you will find a starting point for understanding what Christians mean when they say "God," and to whom they are referring when they use this name. Maybe it should be obvious what we mean when we say this word ("God"), since it is so central to our faith, but we encounter misconceptions about its meaning all the time. And, if we are honest, even we might admit that lurking somewhere in the back of our minds we have an image of God as a nice old man sitting in the sky.

There is, however, sometimes a resistance to thinking about God, especially in a theological or philosophical way. We might protest that we are not smart enough to do theology and that less is more when it comes to contemplating the divine. We might even think that too much theology detracts from simple faith. In fact, we all know people with a strong faith who have not opened a single theology book! But if God is perfect, wonderful, all goodness, love itself—as the Bible tells us in 1 John 4:8—it would be strange indeed if we did not want to give our whole selves to God, including our minds.

The Lord himself, when asked to state the most important commandment, responded: "[Y]ou shall love the Lord your God with all your heart and with all your soul and with all your mind and with all your strength" (Mk 12:30). Jesus is quoting from Deuteronomy 6:5, but he adds the words "with all your mind," making clear to us that we should love God with our whole selves and with all the faculties available to us as human beings. It would be a bad sign in a marriage, after all, if a wife told her husband that after the wedding day she no longer wanted to learn anything more about him, and that knowing too much about him might make her love him less! She would probably end up loving the image of her spouse that she had in her head rather than a real person. Likewise, we should want to love the one true God and not the God of our imagining. And, since God is perfect, knowing more about him can only make us love him more, not less. When we profess faith in God, or experience a conversion to faith, this is not the end of our coming to know God, but the beginning.

It is easy to see at once, moreover, how foggy thinking about God can deeply affect our faith and our ability to communicate it to other people. To take the example of God as an old man: if we think of God, even in the back of our minds, as a giant version of a human being, it is no small wonder that our faith in God remains only a version of our faith in other people. And, we might add, we can see why many people around us reject God out of hand, because they judge God by the standards of human behavior and limitations, and therefore ultimately see God as an invention of the human imagination. Thinking about God as a human being whose power, love, and size have simply been multiplied by a very large number is only one example of how we might think about God in a wrongheaded way. We might think about God as a nebulous force of goodness and happiness in the world, about whom we can say very little in specific terms. Or, we might think that God is roughly equivalent to the Big Bang, that he is the "something" that sets the world in motion, but that he remains at a distance. In these cases, the God of the Bible is a fairy tale and religion has really nothing to do with us or our everyday lives. All of these ways of thinking about God (even if I have exaggerated them) represent ideas that we have encountered or that we ourselves have perhaps even entertained to a greater or lesser degree.

If we want to love God, to serve God, and to make God the center of our lives, we would do well to settle this question at least in some small way: Who is God? What sort of God is the Christian God? To return to the analogy of marriage: when two people intend to get married, they spend time getting to know one another before they pledge to live their lives together. Neither the bride-to-be nor the groom-to-be would be discouraged by the fact that one person can never completely know another. Therefore, if we intend to spend eternity with God, we should also spend some time getting to know something about him. Let us not be discouraged by the fact that God is beyond our complete knowing.

This book will therefore begin by asking what we mean when we say "God." Who does God say that he is in the Bible, and what do we mean when we use words to describe God: words such as "all-knowing" (omniscient), "all-powerful" (omnipotent), "infinite," "eternal," and the like? By attempting to understand our words, we can push ourselves a little further in coming to know what the word "God" means. The term that is often used to refer to the *what* of God is the word "nature." So, we will first consider the nature of God and why it matters for our faith. We will then discuss what is called the doctrine of the Trinity, the uniquely Christian claim that God is three-in-one. When a Catholic professes faith in God, it is in God as Trinity: God as Father, Son, and Holy Spirit. Coming to know God as Trinity is essential to understanding to whom the word "God" is referring. After we have some sense of the *what* of God (the nature of God) and the *who* of God (the Father, Son, and Holy Spirit), we will turn to the Incarnation—that is, we will talk about what it means for God to have become a human being in Jesus Christ. It is only through Christ that we can meet God in the flesh and, therefore, understand the destiny of humankind and our hope of heaven.

Hopefully this book will serve as an occasion for you to love God with your mind, and to equip you to explain the essentials of the faith to others. There are many rich aspects of our Christian faith, but compared to God himself these are nothing. For this reason, in the creed, the first thing we profess is belief in God ("I believe in God, the Father almighty . . . "). Or, as the *Catechism of the Catholic Church* says, "The mystery of the Most Holy Trinity is the central mystery of Christian faith and life. It is the mystery of God in himself. It is therefore the source of all the other mysteries of faith, the light that enlightens them."[1]

---

1   *Catechism of the Catholic Church*, 234 (hereafter cited as *CCC*).

2

God's Name

If we want to understand what a Christian means by the word "God," the best place to start is the Bible. We can hear about a person from others, we can gather information about someone from various sources, but we would not say we know a person unless he speaks with us. Likewise, it is in the Bible where we encounter God and his own words about himself, where we can hear him speak to us and therefore come to know him. One of the most dramatic moments in the Bible when God tells us something about himself is found in Exodus 3, where Moses has the gumption to ask God directly for his name. Moses, at this time, is living as a shepherd in the land of Midian. One day, while he is minding his own business and tending his sheep, he sees something strange—a bush that is on fire and yet is not burning up—and he turns aside to find out what this sign could mean. When he approaches the bush, the voice of God tells him to remove his sandals, for he is standing on holy ground. God then proceeds to introduce himself as the God of Abraham, Isaac, and Jacob and to tell Moses that he has been chosen to lead his people out of slavery in Egypt. Moses is not initially pleased with God's plan. He protests that he is not equal to the task and that no one will believe he has been commissioned by God. Moses then asks for God's credentials—some divine identifier—in order that he might tell the Israelites who has sent him. God's response?

> God said to Moses, "I AM WHO I AM." And he said, "Say this to
> the people of Israel: 'I AM has sent me to you.'" God also said
> to Moses, "Say this to the people of Israel: 'The Lord, the God
> of your fathers, the God of Abraham, the God of Isaac, and the
> God of Jacob, has sent me to you.' This is my name forever, and
> thus I am to be remembered throughout all generations." (Ex
> 3:14–15)

To me, this story is the perfect starting place for our quest to
gain some understanding of God. Let us follow Moses's example
and turn aside for a moment from our daily concerns and allow
ourselves to be drawn in by God's brilliance. And what better
place to begin to understand God than with his own chosen
calling card? "I AM WHO I AM."

What does this name mean? Whatever it means, it
immediately banishes any thought of God as an old man in the
sky, for even the oldest of men would not have a name like this
one. In the Christian tradition, this name has been taken not
only as a true name by which we might call upon God, but also
as God revealing his nature to us in a way that we can understand
it. Remember that the word "nature" refers to *what* God is, the
essence of God and what he can do. The name "I AM WHO I AM"
or simply "I AM" tells us that God is not one living thing among
many things, not one form of existence in the universe that can
be counted with others, but that God *is*. God is life itself, God
exists through himself and not by the power of another, and
without God there is nothing else. God does not change or
pass from doing one thing to another. The God of the burning
bush is "the Father of lights, with whom there is no variation
or shadow due to change" (Jas 1:17). Or, as Hebrews says of
Christ, God is "the same yesterday and today and forever" (Heb
13:8). A philosophical word that is used to capture some of these
ideas about God is the word "transcendent"—it means that God
is not one thing or person in the world, but completely different

from the world, above and beyond it. God is not huge, for he occupies no such thing as space. God is not old, for he passes through no such thing as time. Time and space are dimensions of the created world, which God surpasses, because God is transcendent. God *is*, eternally present and existing.

We might nod our heads and think we have understood this fact about God. Of course, once we have begun to think about it, it may seem obvious that God is beyond all things and not restricted by space or time. But we should not be so hasty to assume that we have grasped the entire meaning of this name in one intellectual swoop. The Israelites seemed to have struggled with it considerably, frequently thinking that their God was just one god among many who, although very powerful, might not be the most worth worshipping (or, at the very least, not the easiest one to worship). For this reason, the prophet Jonah could casually comment that he "fears the God of heaven, who made the sea and the dry land" (Jon 1:9), while at the same time trying to escape that very God in a boat *on the sea*. Jonah seemingly grasps that his God is not an element in the universe but the creator of it, and yet he certainly does not act like it! We too, although we know that God is beyond everything in this world, can act as if we have him completely figured out, whereas, in fact, we will not understand completely until we see God face to face. We will continue to speak about the further implications of God's existence in the following three chapters, but for now let us return to the speech that God made to Moses and to another foundational truth it reveals about God's character: God's name reveals not only that he is *above* all things, but also that he is *present to and in* all things.

If the revealing of God's name demolishes all false notions of God as an elderly man, it should equally demolish any idea of God as a distant watchmaker or impersonal force. God reveals his actual name to a particular human being at a particular location. God's "I am" is not in the first instance a philosophical statement, but it describes God's actions in the Exodus story. In Hebrew, God's name could just as well be in the future tense, and so it could be translated into English as "I will be who I will be." In some sense, then, God's name is a bit of a joke on Moses. Moses has asked God for his name so that he will have a guarantee of success with the Israelites in Egypt, and God responds that his name is "the one who will be with you"! In other words, Moses asks, "Who is going to be there with me in Egypt?" and it is to this question that God responds, "I AM." Moses is told in that name—"I AM"—not simply that God is all-powerful, the source of existence, and so on, but that he truly has God for his ally. God will be with him in any situation. For this reason, God adds a reminder about the past to his promise about the future: Moses is also to tell the people that "I AM" is the God of Abraham, Isaac, and Jacob, and to make sure that they remember his name throughout all generations. One of the facts about God we have just discussed above then, that God does not change, does not make him impersonal or distant, but reliable and present. It is true that God is not one thing in the universe, but God's name also tells us that he is present to all things in the universe, and not merely present as a warm fuzzy feeling or as an all-pervasive force, but present as an actor and cause. From the story in Exodus, we know that God has made that presence and love known in time and space to real people. He is not just the God of the cosmos, but the God of Abraham, Isaac, and Jacob. The word sometimes used to describe this quality of God is "immanent" (not to be confused with "imminent"). Immanent means right here, present, with us.

As with God's transcendence, God's immanence can also seem rather obvious once we have labeled it. Of course God is everywhere present, and we know that the Bible speaks frequently of God's intimate acting in the history of the world. But, once again, this fact about God is one that we need to encounter again and again in order to begin to understand it and live according to it. It is one that we will only know securely by frequent hearing of the Bible and by prayer, because we may know that God acts in history in theory, but we cannot know that he acts in our own lives except by experience. There is nothing more sobering than prayer for helping us come to terms with God's immediacy and his desire to work in the world and in us. For example, although frustrated by great suffering, it is in conversation with God that Job is able to express God's care for him, that God is not a distant creator of the world, but Job's own creator: "You clothed me with skin and flesh, and knit me together with bones and sinews. You have granted me life and steadfast love, and your care has preserved my spirit" (Jb 10:11–12). Likewise, it is often in psalms—which are prayers—that we see a biblical author reflecting on the amazing fact that the God of the universe is also the God of every individual:

> O LORD, you have searched me and known me!
> You know when I sit down and when I rise up;
> you discern my thoughts from afar.
> You search out my path and my lying down
> and are acquainted with all my ways.
> Even before a word is on my tongue,
> behold, O LORD, you know it altogether.
> You hem me in, behind and before,
> and lay your hand upon me.
> Such knowledge is too wonderful for me;
> it is high; I cannot attain it. (Ps 139:1–6)

The psalmist marvels at the God of the universe who knows all things, and praises God not just because he knows all the facts there are to know about the universe, but because God knows each person and what is in our hearts. Let us accordingly follow the advice of 1 Peter, which captures our proper response to the greatness of God and his regard for us in our smallness: "Humble yourselves, therefore, under the mighty hand of God so that at the proper time he may exalt you, casting all your anxieties on him, because he cares for you" (1 Pt 5:6–7). God is certainly a God of the big picture, but that does not prevent him in any way from being a God of the small picture too—because he *is*, he is in all things great and small, he causes all things great and small.

Another wonderful biblical passage that demonstrates that God is in both great and small comes from the vision of the prophet Elijah in 1 Kings. In this passage, Elijah is fleeing Jezebel in fear for his life and has fasted forty days and forty nights when he arrives at Mount Horeb. There God makes his presence known to Elijah in portends of all kinds:

> And behold, the LORD passed by, and a great and strong wind tore the mountains and broke in pieces the rocks before the LORD, but the LORD was not in the wind. And after the wind an earthquake, but the LORD was not in the earthquake. And after the earthquake a fire, but the LORD was not in the fire. And after the fire the sound of a low whisper. (1 Kgs 19:11–12)

Here, Elijah sees awesome signs of the might of God—a terrible wind, earthquake, and fire—but the Lord transcends all these. God is creator and master of these elements of the world. But, after all these terrifying displays of his power, the Lord speaks to Elijah not by thundering from a cloud but in "the sound of a low whisper." In this still, soft voice, God commands Elijah to return to Israel and to continue to act as the prophet that the people of God so desperately need. God, in other words, has a plan for his people (and the whole world), but he still acts through a small voice spoken to a frightened man in the wilderness.

By our study of God's name, and by coming to understand God's transcendence and immanence, therefore, we can see the task set out for us in this book in miniature: to understand how the God of the universe, who is above all, is also the Lord who loves us and comes to us personally. In this way, we can come to appreciate the magnificence of God and yet his nearness to all his creatures.

3

God Exists

In the last chapter, we saw that God is the great "I AM," the source
of all existence. In this chapter, we will ask whether or not this
fact about God, revealed in Scripture, lines up with what we can
know about God from the light of our reason. After all, an ever-
growing number of people reject that God exists in the first place,
let alone see God as his own existence and the ground of all being.
This rejection is, for some, likely based on a false understanding of
God. What self-declared rationalist, for example, would want to
believe in a magical sky man? But as we will see, the name of God
revealed to Moses does not at all offend our reason but satisfies it.
God's self-revelation in the Bible is the first and privileged place
we should look to find out about God, but we must receive that
revelation and explore it with the minds and hearts that God gave
us for this purpose: to know him and to love him. St. Augustine
is known for promoting a definition of doing theology that
complements this way of thinking. For Augustine, theology is
faith seeking understanding. Or, as St. Anselm of Canterbury later
formulates it: "I do not seek to understand in order to believe,
but I believe in order to understand. For I believe even this: that
unless I believe, I shall not understand."[1] Augustine and Anselm

---

1   Anselm of Canterbury, *Proslogion*, in *Complete Philosophical and Theological Treatises of Anselm of Canterbury*, trans. Jasper Hopkins and Herbert Richardson (Minneapolis: Arthur J. Banning Press, 2000), 1.

believe that faith opens up and expands our reason because "we have the mind of Christ" (1 Cor 2:16).

That God is the transcendent cause, and not one thing among many, is confirmed by the traditional proofs for the existence of God. These "proofs" are compelling and logical arguments that convince us to give our assent to their conclusions.

St. Thomas Aquinas famously put forward five proofs for the existence of God in his *Summa Theologiae*, but let us consider just two. The first is the argument from causality. This argument relies on the observation that everything in the universe has a cause. A ball does not move unless someone kicks it. A person cannot be born without parents, and their parents would not exist without their parents and so on. However, this chain of causality cannot go back infinitely without a beginning or starting point. It must lead somewhere. There must be a cause that is unlike all other causes; a cause that is itself uncaused—and this is what we call God. Note that this argument does *not* state that God is the cause of himself. To be a cause, something must first exist, and so not even God can be said to cause himself. For this reason, arguing that the universe caused itself (which some claim is a scientific view) is nonsensical, and does not provide a satisfying answer to the question of causation. Some part of the universe would have to exist before it could cause anything else. Nor does this argument fold to the question: who caused God? The whole premise of the argument is that there must be something—or someone—that is *un*caused for anything else to exist at all. Trying to find the cause of God would be like trying to draw a square with three sides. A square, by definition, has four sides, not only three. God, by definition so to speak, is uncaused. It makes no sense to ask of the uncaused Being, "Who caused him?" This argument from causality therefore leads us to much the same place as the burning bush led Moses. For God to be God he must, by definition, be the cause of all things, not just one cause among many in the universe. It is not, therefore, quite capturing the whole picture to say that God is the one who started up the universe. Rather, it is better to understand that God is the cause of *all* the conditions in the universe that could give rise to its beginning (whether by the Big Bang or in some other way yet to be discovered)—forces, time, space, etc.—because all of these things must be caused. Time and space must be created; they too must have a beginning. In short, the universe must have a cause that exists prior to the universe, and it is therefore logical to conclude that a transcendent cause exists.

The second argument that we will discuss is similar to the first, but perhaps even a little more compelling; it is the argument from contingency. The word "contingent" means something that is not necessary. So, we can say, going to college is contingent on getting admitted. One does not go to college by necessity. Or, we can say it is necessary to have an apple tree in order to grow apples. But if we step back for a moment and think about all of the things in the universe, we can come to see that everything we know and observe is ultimately contingent. I do not *have* to exist. My parents may never have met. Mount Everest does not *have* to exist by necessity; the mountain ranges could well have formed in a different way or someone could go destroy Mount Everest right now with explosives. But if everything in the universe is contingent (meaning that things exist but could very well not exist), then why does anything exist at all? Why is there something rather than nothing? From where do all of these contingent things receive their existence? Once again, we are led to conclude there must be something—or someone—who is not contingent. Something that exists *by necessity*, and this we call God. And what is it that all contingent things cannot do without? They cannot do without existence. It is existence itself that is the necessary thing, which must by definition *be* in order for all other things to receive existence. The one who is necessary is the one who calls himself "I AM"; there must be life itself in order for life to be imparted.

Apart from Aquinas's proofs, there are other proofs for the existence of God that we might understand as proofs from a kind of common sense. For example, C. S. Lewis once wrote that "creatures are not born with desires unless satisfaction for those desires exists. A baby feels hunger: well, there is such a thing as food. A duckling wants to swim: well, there is such a thing as water . . . if I find in myself a desire which no experience in this world could satisfy, the most probable explanation is that I was made for another world."[2] In other words, it is not strange to become thirsty when there is no water in the room, but it would be strange to become thirsty if there were no such thing as water. Unless we are willing to accept that this human desire for something beyond ourselves is nothing but a fantasy or cruel joke, we can take our natural longing for transcendence as an indication of its existence.

Evidence of this human intuition about the existence of something that is beyond the sensible world abounds. If one is inclined to have any respect for the thousands of years of human history that have come before us, one ought to have some regard for religion, because if there is a common language of human expression, it is a religious one. The sociologist Mircea Eliade famously described a human being not so much as *homo sapiens* (a reasoning person) but as *homo religiosus* (a religious person)[3] because of the universal religious character of human beings. To follow C. S. Lewis's logic, this innate human desire to reach out to God, which has been expressed in so many times and places, would be very odd if it represented only a long-standing and widespread delusion. This human intuition about the

---

2   C. S. Lewis, *Mere Christianity* (Harper Collins, 2000), 136–37.

3   Mircea Eliade, *The Quest: History and Meaning in Religion* (1969; repr., Chicago: University of Chicago Press, 1984), 8–9.

transcendent has many expressions and not just in identifiable religion. It is also expressed, for example, in the human desire for morality and justice. We have an intuition, an innate sense, that some things are right and wrong, that some things are good and some are bad. We intuit, for example, that murder is wrong. When we have this sense about murder (among other things), we do not simply understand that murder happens to be inconvenient or destructive to society, but that it is wrong, not to be committed even if there were no larger ramifications. But in order for there to be any kind of morality that is absolute and not just based on personal opinion or the spirit of a particular era, we must allow that there is something absolute and eternal more generally speaking. We have imprinted on our hearts a notion of the divine and a desire to act according to some higher order. To describe this "proof" from human intuition, the *Catechism* says: "The human person: with his openness to truth and beauty, his sense of moral goodness, his freedom and the voice of his conscience, with his longings for the infinite and for happiness, man questions himself about God's existence. In all this he discerns signs of his spiritual soul."[4]

Whether we start from the Bible, philosophical reasoning, or from human intuition, we arrive at a similar conclusion: there is something more than the visible world. There is transcendence. As St. Paul says: "[W]hat can be known about God is plain to them, because God has shown it to them. For his invisible attributes, namely, his eternal power and divine nature, have been clearly perceived, ever since the creation of the world, in the things that have been made" (Rom 1:19–20). We can, from our knowledge of the world, perceive and confirm what the Scriptures have also revealed. In Exodus 3, we learn that this transcendence is not an impersonal force but the God of Abraham, Isaac, and Jacob—the one who names himself "I

---

4   *CCC*, 33.

AM" because he is the ground of all being. God's self-revelation is corroborated by the observations made by Aquinas (and other philosophers before him) that there must be a cause of the universe unlike other causes; the uncaused cause and the unmoved mover. This cause, moreover, cannot be seen as merely impersonal, because it implies a Mind that orders and creates. These biblical and philosophical observations about the existence of God also correspond to our own human intuition about God, one that many of us have experienced in our own hearts, but that can also be observed throughout human history. It is, therefore, satisfying to our reason to conclude that God exists and is the source of existence.

4

God's Nature

Having discussed the name of God and its meaning, we are now in a better position to answer more fully a question posed in the introduction: What is God? What can we say about God's nature? The first and most important thing we can say about God's nature is that it is *one*. That God is one is essential to our faith. In Deuteronomy 6, Moses includes an affirmation of God's oneness as an integral part of the greatest commandment:

> Hear, O Israel: The LORD our God, the LORD is one. You shall love the LORD your God with all your heart and with all your soul and with all your might. And these words that I command you today shall be on your heart. You shall teach them diligently to your children, and shall talk of them when you sit in your house, and when you walk by the way, and when you lie down, and when you rise. (Dt 6:4–7)

Deuteronomy 6:4 ("Hear, O Israel: The LORD our God, the LORD is one"), the *shema*, remains central to Jewish liturgy and prayer to this day, according to Moses's instruction to pass on these words diligently and to speak of them constantly. Moses proclaims that understanding God's oneness is the first step to being able to love God with all your heart, all your soul, and all your might. But why? Firstly, monotheism is fundamental to proper worship. If we believed not in one God but many, we might go searching for other divinities or chasing after what appears to be a god (something that in fact happens repeatedly in the Old Testament!). In short, if we have more than one god, we cannot love the true God with our whole self.

But the oneness of God is also essential for understanding the other attributes of God, such as his omnipotence (his almightiness). If there is more than one god, after all, then the God of the Bible cannot be all mighty. God cannot have any competitors if he is truly the transcendent God about whom we have been speaking. Likewise, if God is to be understood as the uncaused cause, then he must be unique, and he must precede all other things that could be considered a cause. Therefore, to be the God revealed in Exodus and defined as he is by Aquinas, God must be one.

God's oneness, as stated in the *shema*, however, is not just a declaration of monotheism. It is not merely a statement about God being the only God that there is. It is also a statement about the simplicity of God. To be omnipotent, God must be the only one, but his oneness also helps us to understand the true meaning of omnipotence. Because, if we now understand that God is not just a giant version of a human being, we must also understand how being all-powerful is not the same as having human power amplified. To be *all* powerful, God must have no limitations either internally or externally. God, therefore, cannot be divided up into parts or aspects, which would be an internal limitation or demarcation. God also cannot have any outward boundaries or limitations; hence God is eternal (not bound by time) and infinite (not bound by space). God therefore cannot change, as he does not move or develop. Since God always *is*, he cannot change from what he is at the moment to what he potentially could be. This simplicity of God also means there is no distinction between what God is, what he has, and what he does. We have discussed some of these terms already when we were speaking of God's transcendence, but here we can see these attributes of God are grounded in his one, whole, and simple nature. We have begun with the name of God as the great "I AM" and can now see how all of the common words we use to describe God make sense: God is his own existence, which means that he is one—both unique and simple. What follows is that God is all-powerful, all-knowing, eternal, infinite, unchanging, and incorporeal. St. Augustine has a pithy phrase for capturing these truths about God: "[Y]ou are everywhere whole" (*ubique totus es*);[1] here we have a summary of God's transcendence, immanence, simplicity, and limitlessness. In a word, God is perfect.

Laying out these seemingly abstract terms for the nature of God has important implications for other kinds of words we use to describe God and his relationship to us: for example, God as creator. Since we know that God is simple and entire, when we speak about God creating, we also know that creation does not give God anything that he lacks, nor does it change God. By understanding the nature of God, therefore, we can come to see creation for the completely gratuitous, free, and selfless act that it is. God created us for our own sake and not for any gain or progress of his own, because he is perfect and possesses his existence perfectly. And, although we change in time, we know that God's plans for creation have never changed. In Genesis 1, when the process of creation is described, we are never given a reason for creation. God has no hidden agenda—we are told only that what God created was good. Understanding this fact about creation changes everything. It makes us aware of the great gift of life and the beauty of the cosmos, for which we can pay nothing other than gratitude. When we understand God for who he is and creation for what it is, we can begin to learn to live our lives

---

1   *The Confessions of Saint Augustine,* trans. John K. Ryan (New York: Doubleday, 1960), 1.1.4.

in an attitude of thankfulness; we can learn to begrudge others nothing and to be satisfied with what we have. For this reason, many psalms of praise are praises of creation. We do not only owe God thanks for this or that good thing, but for all good things that receive from God their very existence. Psalm 148 is a particularly beautiful example, as it calls on the creatures of God (from highest to lowest) to turn to him who made them what they are:

> Praise the LORD!
> Praise the LORD from the heavens;
> > praise him in the heights!
> Praise him, all his angels;
> > praise him, all his hosts!
>
> Praise him, sun and moon,
> > praise him, all you shining stars!
> Praise him, you highest heavens,
> > and you waters above the heavens!
>
> Let them praise the name of the LORD!
> > For he commanded and they were created.
> And he established them forever and ever;
> > he gave a decree, and it shall not pass away. (Ps 148:1–6)

Knowing that God is perfect helps us to appreciate the life he has given to us out of no need of his own, and also the perfection that he offers to us, a perfection that "shall not pass away" because God's decree is unchanging. The whole earth can praise God in harmony because all of the diversity of the natural world is produced by one who is simple.

In a similar vein, when we have a proper understanding of God as the uncaused cause and we see the true meaning of his omnipotence, we can also see that God is not in competition with the universe. Sometimes in modern discourse about religion and science, people have an either/or mentality about causality. *Either* the Big Bang caused the universe *or* God caused the universe. *Either* someone's disease was healed by medical intervention *or* God cured it. But since we know that God's almightiness extends everywhere always and that he is present to his whole creation, and since we know that he is not one cause among many in the universe, we should instead adopt a both/and way of thinking about causality. Saying "God causes a tree to grow" does not in any way exclude the natural causes for a tree to grow (light, water, etc.) because God does not compete with his own universe; rather, he works in and through it. It is an impoverished view of God to think that to be powerful he must violate or go against the laws and structures of the universe that he himself created. As we have been discussing, God is not just very powerful (as we might think of human power), exerting his own will on others by force. Instead, God is all powerful, the sustainer and worker of all things.

There are many examples in the Bible that demonstrate that God's agency is not in competition with other agents and causes, because he is the unique first principle. We often encounter people in the biblical narrative who are acting both according to God's will and yet by their own will as well. For example, in the story of Joseph found in Genesis 37–50, we see many people doing many different things (some of which do not turn out very well for Joseph!), but we also know that God is working through them. First, Joseph's brothers decide to kill him out of jealousy, but then change their minds and instead sell him into slavery in Egypt. Joseph's master in Egypt soon turns against him because of a false accusation and he is sent to prison. But then, Joseph's ability to interpret dreams (which he showcases to his fellow inmates) earns him a promotion to Pharaoh's right-hand man. Eventually Joseph's brothers come to Egypt seeking relief in a time of famine, but they do not recognize their long-lost brother when they ask him for help. After testing them, Joseph is reconciled to them and reunites with his father. Throughout this whole narrative, however, God is hardly mentioned, and none of the events are directly attributed to God's power—until the end of the story. Joseph explains that it was not his brothers who had sent him to Egypt but rather God and that God had ordained all of the events, which had taken place for a greater good. To allay the fear of his repentant brothers that he might be vengeful, Joseph declares: "As for you, you meant evil against me, but God meant it for good" (Gn 50:20). Joseph does not mean by this statement that his brothers lost their free will or that God was controlling them while they were unaware, but rather that God is powerful enough to work in and through the truly free actions of his brothers. God can be the cause of Joseph's redemption without eliminating the other causes at work in the story.

Understanding something about the nature of God, therefore, helps us understand what it means for God to be our creator. But knowing that God is simple, infinite, eternal, and the like can also help us understand how God can be all-loving, all-forgiving, and just. God's love, like his power, is beyond all human love. It does not change, it can extend to all people and places, it can touch everything in the universe simultaneously. Likewise, God's forgiveness and his justice are based on his full understanding of every single thing—no matter how bad— and of every circumstance that has prevented us from living better than we have. God's forgiveness, therefore, is complete; there are never any false pretenses or misunderstandings when it comes to God's knowledge of our hearts and his ability to heal them. Because we know that God is the source of life, we know that God is capable of restoring us to fullness of life. He can renew us and remake us because he is our maker.

A memorable image of the relationship between God's love and his power comes from Ezekiel 37. In this chapter, God shows Ezekiel a vision with a valley full of dry bones. God asks Ezekiel, "Son of man, can these bones live?" and Ezekiel confesses the power and wisdom of God, answering, "O Lord God, you know" (Ez 37:3). God then tells Ezekiel to preach to these dry bones, and he hears "a rattling," and the bones coming together, "bone to its bone" (Ez 37:7); flesh comes upon the bones again and God breathes into them the breath of life (Ez 37:8–9). God tells Ezekiel that these bones signify the lost house of Israel, which at present has no hope or life. It is to Israel that God has sent Ezekiel with the promise that the people will be restored. This vision shows us once again that God is the giver of life, the "I am" who alone imparts existence. But God's power is shown forth in this vision not simply because he can raise the dead, but because the dead he is raising are his own beloved people who have turned from him and betrayed him. God's display of power is therefore also a sign of his steadfast love, and a beautiful reminder of the transforming power of God's forgiveness. God forgives not in the sense that God ignores bad things that have happened, but rather his forgiveness is truly life-giving and healing.

Now we have come to a preliminary answer to the first question that we have been posing in this book: *what is God?* The Lord our God is one, unique, simple, and perfect, which means he is also omnipotent, omniscient, eternal, and infinite. These attributes are in no way separate from his love and his mercy; rather, understanding truths about the nature of God helps us to understand even more clearly how powerful and all-encompassing his love and mercy are, and how we can rely on them completely. As the psalmist sings, "Give thanks to the God of heaven, for his steadfast love endures forever" (Ps 136:26); it is only a transcendent God who can give us the truly everlasting love we seek.

5

Speaking about God

We have thus far been speaking about the nature of God, as well as the kinds of words we use to describe God. But perhaps, having now come to terms (to some degree) with the transcendence of God, a doubt is creeping into your mind, a doubt about whether it is even possible to speak about God in the first place. If God is really infinite—unbound both internally and externally—how can we possibly describe him with finite words? And it is in fact true that no words can fully describe God because he is infinite, eternal, without bounds, unknowable in his entirety. The specific word used for this quality of God is "ineffable." God cannot be adequately described. And, as much as the Bible tells us about God, it also asserts that God is unknowable and beyond us. At the end of the book of Job, for example, after Job has made long petitions to God to relieve his pain, after he has questioned God and endured the lengthy discourses of his friends, he finally receives a divine response to his questions. God answers Job: "Shall a faultfinder contend with the Almighty? He who argues with God, let him answer it" (Jb 40:2). God goes on to point out how limited Job's knowledge is in comparison to divine knowledge, how the works of God are so unlike human works, and how God's power exceeds human imagination. Job must therefore respond as the finite human being that he is: "I have uttered what I did not understand, things too wonderful for me, which I did not know" (Jb 42:3). Likewise, when St. Paul is wrestling to understand human free will and divine providence in the letter to the Romans, he turns aside to cry out:

> Oh, the depth of the riches and wisdom and knowledge of God! How unsearchable are his judgments and how inscrutable his ways! "For who has known the mind of the Lord, or who has been his counselor? Or who has given a gift to him that he might be repaid?"(Rom 11:33–35)

Paul, like Job, expresses the limitation of his knowledge in the face of the transcendent, unknowable God.

Well, so much for this book and all that we have been doing so far! But do not despair so quickly. From the outset, we have acknowledged this fact about God. We know that God is a mystery. And although God is a mystery much greater than the mystery of the human person, coming to know him more and more is analogous to coming to know someone we love ever more deeply. Indeed, St. Augustine understands our human efforts to speak about God as an act of worship. He writes that although "nothing really worthy of God can be said about him, he has accepted the homage of human voices and has wished us to rejoice in praising him with our words."[1] God not only tolerates our speaking about him, but wishes for us to speak of him—as evidenced by his having given us the Bible in the first place, and his having spoken with many people. So, on the one hand, we should never give up coming to know God and speaking of him. But, on the other, we should acknowledge the limitations that we have when it comes to speaking about God. Therefore, let us

---

1   Augustine, *Teaching Christianity: De Doctrina Christiana,* trans. Edmund Hill (Hyde Park, N.Y.: New City Press, 1996), 1.6.

now briefly consider in what way our words are able to give some expression to who God is.

One way in which we tend to speak about God, which avoids the problem of not being able to say anything directly about the divine nature, is to speak apophatically. The word "apophatic" is Greek and comes from a verb that means "to speak in the negative" or "to deny." Apophatic words do not attempt to say what God *is* but only limit themselves to saying what God is *not*. Therefore, by negation, we can get a kind of shadow or photo negative image of the nature of God, which is indescribable. Many of the words used in the previous chapter fall into this category of apophatic words. For example, the word "infinite." In-finite simply means "not finite" or "having no end." The word "infinite" does not say exactly what the opposite of being finite or limited is; it only asserts that God is *not finite* and is without end. Another example would be "incorporeal." In-corporeal means "not having a body." Saying that God is incorporeal does not therefore assert what God *has*, but what he does *not* have. There are many other similar words we use to speak about God: immortal (i.e., not mortal), immutable (i.e., not mutating, not changing), invisible (i.e., not visible), and even the word "ineffable" itself (i.e., not utterable, unspeakable).

Employing negative words and concepts as a starting point for the contemplation of God has been, for many in the Christian tradition, a way of mystical or spiritual ascent. By thinking of something we know and then negating it, we can ascend step by step into experiencing how different God is from us. The ascent to God by way of negation or denial is sometimes understood as lingering in darkness, knowing the light by its absence, or as "seeing" God but in a cloud (the cloud being a common sign of the presence of God in Scripture). The glory of the Lord appears as a cloud prominently in Exodus, where God indicates his presence by a cloud descending on the tabernacle to tell the Israelites whether to stay or to travel (see Ex 40:34–38). But this image is also found in the New Testament. For example, at the transfiguration when Peter, James, and John see Jesus appear in all his glory, and a bright cloud overshadows Jesus, finally concealing the one who speaks: "This is my beloved Son, with whom I am well pleased" (Mt 17:5). The disciples fall on their faces because they cannot look directly at the divine presence. An anonymous late fourteenth-century text called *The Cloud of Unknowing* describes this process of searching for God in the darkness:

> The darkness and cloud is always between you and your God no matter what you do, and it prevents you from seeing him clearly by the light of understanding in your reason and from experiencing him in the sweetness of love in your affection. So set yourself to rest in this darkness as long as you can, always crying out after him whom you love.[2]

This author seems to paint a rather grim picture of the search for God with our human reason, but he is not speaking so differently from Augustine, because seeking after God despite our limitations is the way in which we worship and love God. It is also helpful to keep always in mind, like the author of *The Cloud*, the fact that in this life we can never see God as he is. It makes our struggle to understand him and our times of suffering more comprehensible, and even an integral part of our spiritual journey. Learning to seek for God in spiritual darkness and to feel his presence by his absence can be very useful to us in times of spiritual dryness or doubt. Mother Teresa famously experienced this sort of spiritual darkness for many years, but, like the author of *The Cloud*, learned to cry

---

2   *The Cloud of Unknowing*, ed. James Walsh, S.J. (New York: Paulist Press, 1981), 3.

out after God in her desolation and even to understand Christ better because of it. Of this experience she writes: "I have come to love the darkness—for I now believe it is a very, very small part of Jesus' darkness and pain on earth."[3]

However, despite the exhortation of *The Cloud of Unknowing* to seek God in the darkness and our myriad experiences of spiritual blindness, we nevertheless do use many positive words to describe God as well, such as when we say that God is good or that God is merciful. We must acknowledge first that because God is one and simple, as discussed in the last chapter, these qualities of God that we multiply for our own understanding are, in God himself, identical. In other words, God's mercy *is* his justice *is* his love *is* his being. In God, these are not different attributes because God does not have aspects or parts. Nevertheless, when *we* say that God is merciful, we do not mean exactly the same thing as saying that God is just. Can we therefore be saying anything meaningful about God at all? The answer, according to Aquinas, is yes! And if we believe the Bible really says anything true about God when it applies positive characteristics to him, we will agree. When we speak about God, our words do not describe him completely, so they are not "univocal," says Aquinas. But, when we speak of God, we also do not mean something completely different than what those words mean to us on earth, so the words are also not "equivocal." Equivocation in language occurs when the same word means two completely different things in different contexts. For example, compare "let me go check on the baby" to "let me write you a check." Although the word "check" appears in both cases, in one case it is a verb meaning to look or examine and in the other case it is a noun meaning a piece

---

3   Mother Teresa, *Come Be My Light: The Private Writings of the Saint of Calcutta,* ed. Brian Kolodiejchuk (New York: Doubleday, 2007), 208.

of paper that you can use to transfer money to someone. In this example, there is an equivocation of the word "check."

Aquinas's solution to the problem of how to understand in what way our language applies to God is to say that words used of God are neither univocal nor equivocal but *analogous*; our words express something similar to, but not identical with, the divine nature. To understand how language about God can be analogous, let's take an everyday example of our use of language. When we say "These socks are dirty," we do not mean exactly the same thing by "dirty" as in the sentence "You're a dirty liar," and yet we do not mean something entirely different, either. There is a sharing of meaning in the concept of uncleanliness, although one is physical and the other is not. Likewise, when we speak of God, we really can say something true of him, even if what we say can never capture the entirety of that truth. Metaphorical or imaginative language appears constantly in the Bible, and, indeed, we will never understand the Bible at all, nor the God of the Bible, if we are not comfortable with images, stories, and analogies. These images in the biblical text, however, often strike a balance between being ones that we can understand and yet also being strange enough that we can resist the temptation to bring God down to our own level. This use of powerful images is especially striking in the prophets and in the book of Revelation. We are often told that the prophet saw something that had the *likeness* of something else, prompting us to think about the Bible's use of language in this realm of analogy. For example, in Ezekiel 1, the prophet has an intense vision of God traveling on a chariot covered in eyes and guided by heavenly beings. When the prophet describes the appearance of the one seated on the throne (the closest thing to seeing God himself), the word "likeness" appears many times:

> And above the expanse over their heads there was the likeness
> of a throne, in appearance like sapphire; and seated above the

likeness of a throne was a likeness with a human appearance. And upward from what had the appearance of his waist I saw as it were gleaming metal, like the appearance of fire enclosed all around. And downward from what had the appearance of his waist I saw as it were the appearance of fire, and there was brightness around him. Like the appearance of the bow that is in the cloud on the day of rain, so was the appearance of the brightness all around. (Ez 1:26–28)

Through this piling on of images—of fire, gemstones, metal, brightness, and a rainbow—we can get a glimpse of the glory of God that Ezekiel encountered, and yet we are in no way deceived into thinking that God's glory is roughly equivalent to a sapphire. Likewise, when we say "God is good" (for example), we really do mean something. We have an experience of goodness in this life that is not wholly unlike the goodness that God is, and yet God's goodness will always exceed our understanding. Aquinas puts it this way: "[W]hen we say, 'God is good,' the meaning is not, 'God is the cause of goodness,' or 'God is not evil;' but the meaning is, 'Whatever good we attribute to creatures, pre-exists in God and in a higher way.'"[4]

This distinction of Aquinas is worth bearing in mind when we read through the Scriptures and wrestle with its many images and ways of speaking. The Bible is written for us, adjusted to our language, and speaks through the created things to which we are accustomed. Thus God is sometimes described in an anthropomorphic way, meaning that God is described as acting like a human being or having human traits. These anthropomorphic images help us to learn things about God that we might not otherwise understand, and they

---

4   Thomas Aquinas, *Summa Theologiae* (Lander, Wyo.: Aquinas Institute for the Study of Sacred Doctrine, 2012), I, q. 13, a. 2.

maintain the balance between familiar and strange, which prompts us to seek him further. For example, in the story of the Fall found in Genesis 3, we are told that Adam and Eve "heard the sound of the LORD God walking in the garden in the cool of the day" (Gn 3:8). The use of this language does not negate other passages that make clear God's transcendence and incorporeality. Perhaps this is best demonstrated by the fact that Genesis 1 is a markedly different creation story from Genesis 2–3. The first story (Genesis 1) uses language that helps us understand God's transcendence. It tells of a God who creates everything in the beginning. It speaks of a heavenly order of seven days and depicts a God with complete command over everything in the universe. In this first story, God creates by a simple word. The second story (Genesis 2–3), however, attributes to God more human characteristics, enabling us to envision his immanence. For example, God creates Adam by forming him from the dust, and he is said to plant a garden. To return to Genesis 3:8, there is clearly a beauty in the description of God's nearness to Adam and Eve in the image of him walking in the garden in the evening, and also a hint at the evening that has come due to their sin. What we say of God using human language is true: God was near to Adam and Eve as one walking with them, and he called out to them as he does to all sinners. But, these truths flow from God and are true of him in a higher way than we can express. To use Aquinas's distinction, we should not assume that the language of God walking, for example, is univocal—that the term "walking" is used of God in exactly the same way that it is used of a human being.

Perhaps it might seem as if this distinction in language should have been made at the outset, but until we had some idea of the transcendence of God and the majesty we were undertaking to understand, the question of language may have seemed relatively unimportant. But there is another reason that our discussion of language appears here. Beginning in the next chapter, we are going to take a further step toward understanding God, which will require our language to be bent to its extreme: we will begin to discuss the doctrine of the Trinity. It is important to bear in mind as we discuss this doctrine that, on the one hand, our language will always fall short, but that, on the other hand, we can never work hard enough to make our language more precise. It was in an effort to articulate the biblical character of God in the most careful terms possible that specific language for describing the Trinity developed in the tradition of the Church—specific language that appears, for example, in the creed. So, as we move on to our chapters on the Trinity, let us keep in mind the limitations of our language but also remember that our earnest attempts to speak of God are acts of worship.

6

God as Trinity in the Bible

In the last chapter, we discussed our use of language and the adaptation of the Bible to our human understanding in order to pave the way for a contemplation of the Trinity. The doctrine of the Trinity is the Christian doctrine that God is triune, or three-in-one. Given the emphasis we have been placing on the oneness and transcendence of God in the previous chapters, this claim should give us pause! Many early Christians who were trained in philosophy struggled to understand and even to accept this mystery. But, although it seemed to run against a classical understanding of monotheism, early Christians professed faith in the Trinity because they found it was taught by Christ (and so also in the Bible), and they maintained that belief in the doctrine of the Trinity was necessary to preserve the true identity of Jesus. In this chapter, we will explore some of the biblical texts that teach us to understand God as being both one and three.

One of the most important passages for understanding the doctrine of the Trinity is the prologue to the Gospel of John. Here, the opening lines of the Gospel echo the opening lines of the book of Genesis, teaching us that a deeper reality about creation is now available to us because of the coming of Christ. This is how the Gospel of John begins:

> In the beginning was the Word, and the Word was with God,
> and the Word was God. He was in the beginning with God. All
> things were made through him, and without him was not any
> thing made that was made. (Jn 1:1–3)

Here, the Gospel is speaking about the creation of the world.
God created by his word. In Genesis 1, we will indeed find that
the mode of God's creation is through speaking. For example, the
first day of creation is described in this way: "And God *said*, 'Let
there be light,' and there was light" (Gn 1:3). The importance of
this may not be at all apparent at first. God created by speaking,
but what difference does that make? Of course God commands
something to be done and it is done! But if we take a moment to
consider this fact a little further, we should perhaps find it a little
odd. For instance, God does not have a mouth. And before the
creation of the world, what language could he be speaking? If the
word he spoke in order to create was audible, in what medium
could it have been heard and by whom? There would be no air to
carry the sound or ears to hear his voice. You might have noticed
that, in the translation cited above, "Word" is capitalized. The
translator is indicating to us that John is speaking not of the
world being created through an audible word made by the
vibration of vocal chords, but through the eternal Word, hence
why John says "the Word was God" and why the Word acts as
a "he" rather than an "it." According to John, the Word is a
person, a divine person. John goes on in the prologue to say that
it was the divine Word who "became flesh and dwelt among
us" (Jn 1:14) in the person of Jesus Christ. We are therefore
left asking the question: If there is only one God, how can there
also be a divine Word who is a person? Or, to put the question
a different way, how can the Word *be* God but also *with* God?

In light of John's re-presentation of Genesis 1, if we return
to the creation story itself, we will find some more traces that
point us toward the plurality of God. Not only does God create

by his Word, but there is another agent present right at the very beginning. We are told that before God begins his creating act "the Spirit of God was hovering over the face of the waters" (Gn 1:2). Although nothing had yet been created, God was there with his Word and his Spirit. Likewise, a little later, when God creates humankind on the sixth day, God speaks of himself in the plural: "God said, 'Let us make man in our image, after our likeness'" (Gn 1:26). This use of the plural could be simply a peculiarity of the Hebrew language, but considering what is revealed in John's Gospel, Christians have seen in this type of language and in this very linguistic peculiarity a hint of the doctrine of the Trinity. The one God speaks of himself as if he were not alone. When reading the prologue of John in tandem with Genesis 1, we are immediately confronted with the difficulty and profundity of the doctrine of the Trinity. Somehow the Word who became flesh is God, and is equal to the God of creation. It is this God, who refers to himself in the plural, after whose image we are made. We can immediately see then that the question of God's identity is not some intellectual math problem (i.e., is God one or three or five?), but a question of who God is, who Christ is, and what it means to be made in the image of God.

These kinds of statements about the relation of Christ the Word to God the Father are not limited to John's prologue only. Throughout the Gospel of John, we find Christ explaining his relationship to the Father in more explicit terms than we find anywhere else in the New Testament. And, as in the prologue, we can see that Christ's relationship to the Father is essential for us to understand God's intended relationship with us. For example, in John 10, Jesus is challenged by some in the temple to speak plainly about his identity. He answers them:

> I told you, and you do not believe. The works that I do in my
> Father's name bear witness about me, but you do not believe

because you are not among my sheep. My sheep hear my voice, and I know them, and they follow me. I give them eternal life, and they will never perish, and no one will snatch them out of my hand. My Father, who has given them to me, is greater than all, and no one is able to snatch them out of the Father's hand. I and the Father are one. (Jn 10:25–30)

In this passage, Jesus speaks plainly in declaring that he is one with God the Father; he is the divine Word of the prologue. Jesus's reason for saying this, however, is not to introduce a philosophical perplexity regarding the nature of God. It is to explain to those present that in and through his works we can truly understand the plan and purpose of the Father. Christ's unity with the Father is also the reason that Christ can offer to his followers everlasting life. The promise of life can only be vouchsafed, as we know from our previous discussion, by him who is Life himself. Christ therefore reaffirms his identity as the Word of God who is also God, because he is the voice that we must follow in order to gain heaven.

A similar passage appears in John 17. In this part of John's Gospel, Jesus is preparing for his death and praying for his disciples in anticipation of the difficulties they will face after his passion. But he also prays for all Christians, and Christ's deepest desire for his followers is that they may share in the unity that he has with his Father,

that they may all be one, just as you, Father, are in me, and I in you, that they also may be in us, so that the world may believe that you have sent me. The glory that you have given me I have given to them, that they may be one even as we are one, I in them and you in me, that they may become perfectly one, so that the world may know that you sent me and loved them even as you loved me. (Jn 17:20–23)

Here, Jesus once again explains that he and the Father are perfectly one. His reason for revealing this relationship is to demonstrate the kind of unity Christians are to have with one another and with God. This unity with Christ is the basis upon which the world will know the Gospel, that is, how the world will know that God has sent his Son to share with us his perfect love. For John, understanding how Christ is one with the Father and yet also one with us is essential to understanding Jesus's mission. To know the details of God's innermost life is also to know the nature of the relationship into which we are invited by God.

John's Gospel is by no means the only place where we might look to have a deeper understanding of this new revelation about God's inner life, namely, that God is one and yet somehow the Word is one with him. There are many other places in the New Testament where we are presented with this teaching. Take, for instance, the introductions to the letters of Paul. We can tend to pass over these formulaic passages when we are reading them or when they are proclaimed at church. Take, for example, the opening of the letter to the Philippians, which is very typical of the letters of Paul: "Grace to you and peace from God our Father and the Lord Jesus Christ" (Phil 1:2). In this opening salutation and others like it, Paul sends his greetings and prayers for grace from both God the Father and Jesus Christ. Paul is a well-educated Jew, "circumcised on the eighth day, of the people of Israel, of the tribe of Benjamin, a Hebrew of Hebrews" (Phil 3:5) by his own account. He knows the teaching of the Old Testament about the unity and oneness of God. And yet, he frequently pairs greetings from Christ with greetings from God the Father without missing a beat. He gives to Christ the title *kyrios* (Lord), which would have been the same word used for God the Father in the Greek translation of the Old Testament commonly read by Jews in Paul's day. In the same letter to the Philippians, Paul also quotes an early Christian hymn that, like the prologue to John's Gospel, proclaims Christ's eternal existence and describes his becoming flesh:

> Christ Jesus, who, though he was in the form of God, did not count equality with God a thing to be grasped, but emptied himself, by taking the form of a servant, being born in the likeness of men. Being found in human form, he humbled himself by becoming obedient to the point of death, even death on a cross. (Phil 2:6–8)

Paul, like the Gospel of John, leaves us asking how to express the relation of Christ with the Father in a way that maintains the oneness of God while at the same time acknowledging the divinity of Christ.

The other Gospels also present us with a Christ who is one with God the Father and yet somehow not identical with him. A way in which this is apparent is in the fact that Christ prays. If Christ prays, to whom is he praying? Surely he prays to the Father and not to himself. And yet, he also displays the power to act only as God can. Such a tension is displayed in Mark's brief account of Jesus walking on the water. At the beginning of this story, Jesus withdraws by himself in order to pray, demonstrating that Jesus is not merely playacting, for the benefit of others, when he prays, but taking time on his own to speak with the Father. The disciples, meanwhile, get into a boat in order to cross the sea. Mark continues:

> And when evening came, the boat was out on the sea, and he was alone on the land. And he saw that they were making headway painfully, for the wind was against them. And about the fourth watch of the night he came to them, walking on the sea. He meant to pass by them, but when they saw him walking on the

sea they thought it was a ghost, and cried out, for they all saw him
and were terrified. But immediately he spoke to them and said,
"Take heart; it is I. Do not be afraid." And he got into the boat
with them, and the wind ceased. (Mk 6:47–51)

Although Jesus prays and is distinct from his Father, almost
immediately after his prayer, Jesus acts as a divine person; this
is apparent in a number of ways. First, we have a mention
of Jesus intending to pass the disciples by. This odd detail
reminds us of appearances of God in the Old Testament,
where God cannot be seen directly. More specifically it seems
to echo Exodus 33, where Moses asks to see God's glory. God
tells Moses that no one can see his face and live, but that the
glory of the Lord can "pass by" Moses as he stands in the cleft
of a rock, and he will be permitted to see the "back" of the
Lord (Ex 33:22–23). A divine appearance is therefore signaled
by Jesus intending to pass the disciples by, and an intimate
encounter with God promised by the fact that he instead stops
alongside of the boat. Secondly, Christ refers to himself using
the name of God from Exodus 3, which we discussed at length
in chapter 2. What is translated, in English, as "It is I" in
Mark 6:50 comes from the same Greek phrase for "I AM" (*ego
eimi*). Jesus calms his disciples' fear of death by proclaiming
himself to be the Life. Lastly, Jesus stills the storm, exhibiting
a control over the world proper to its creator.

From the Gospel of John, then, we are told directly about
the divinity of the Word and the unity of Father and Son.
In Paul's letters, the equality of Father and Son is strongly
suggested and seems even to be assumed by the communities
to whom Paul is writing. We can also see the Father-Son
relationship from other Gospel stories, in the way that Jesus
acts as divine and yet not as identical to the Father. There are
many other biblical passages upon which we could meditate
in order to understand the doctrine of the Trinity, but let

us consider one more that was especially important for early Christian discussions of the matter: the baptism of Jesus and Jesus's subsequent command for us to baptize others. It is in these passages where the identity of the Holy Spirit, about whom we have spoken only a little, is most clear. At Jesus's baptism, his identity as Son is named and the Holy Spirit's place within God's life is revealed. Take, for example, the account of the baptism in Matthew's Gospel:

> Then Jesus came from Galilee to the Jordan to John, to be baptized by him. John would have prevented him, saying, "I need to be baptized by you, and do you come to me?" But Jesus answered him, "Let it be so now, for thus it is fitting for us to fulfill all righteousness." Then he consented. And when Jesus was baptized, immediately he went up from the water, and behold, the heavens were opened to him, and he saw the Spirit of God descending like a dove and coming to rest on him; and behold, a voice from heaven said, "This is my beloved Son with whom I am well pleased." (Mt 3:13–17)

Here, John the Baptist prepares us to understand that Jesus's baptism is not one for the forgiveness of his sins, but something even greater (according to Jesus, a fulfillment of righteousness). When Jesus's baptism is completed, we see a dramatic unveiling of his identity. He is called the beloved Son of God, and the Spirit descends upon him as the sign of the truth of his Sonship. The Holy Spirit's descent is also understood as an anointing of Christ, which shows he is the true priest, prophet, and king—those whom the Spirit anointed or came upon in the Old Testament. In this scene, the Father, Son, and Holy Spirit are in communion and work as one to reveal Christ's saving mission. And, by being baptized, Jesus also inaugurates the possibility for us to join that communion by our own baptism. God's inner life, revealed to us at Jesus's baptism, is definitively offered to all people at the end of Matthew's Gospel. It is here where Jesus commissions the disciples to preach the Gospel to all nations, "baptizing them in the name of the Father and of the Son and of the Holy Spirit, teaching them to observe all that I have commanded you" (Mt 28:19–20). Being baptized in the name of the Father, Son, and Holy Spirit is being baptized into the life of God. It would, after all, be very odd to be baptized into the name of the Father and two other, lesser powers. How strange would it be, for example, to be baptized into the name of the Father, the Son, and St. Paul? This baptismal formula indicated to early Christians perhaps most strongly of all biblical passages the equality of the three in the Godhead, and their unity in bringing about human salvation.

Likewise, at the end of John's Gospel, Christ breathes on his disciples the Holy Spirit, because he is the one through whom the disciples continue to share in Christ's mission and purpose: "Jesus said to them again, 'Peace be with you. As the Father has sent me, even so I am sending you.' And when he had said this, he breathed on them and said to them, 'Receive the Holy Spirit'" (Jn 20:22). As the Spirit hovers over the waters of creation (Gn 1:2) and as Adam and Eve received life by God's breath (Gn 2:7), so God's breath, the Holy Spirit, imparts new life to the followers of Christ. Unless the Holy Spirit is divine, and completely united with both Father and Son, he cannot unite us fully to Christ's mission nor impart life, as God is the life-giver.

These biblical passages taken together present us with God's revelation about himself, and the revelation about the life God wants to share with us. God is one, he is eternal life itself. And yet, God emptied himself and came among us as Jesus Christ, and he teaches us that he is not isolated or alone. The life he shares with us by impressing his image upon us is a communal one, and the life the Father offered through Christ comes to us by the Spirit. To grapple with these biblical mysteries, the Christian tradition has developed a way of speaking about God as both one and three, as Father, Son, and Holy Spirit, and this is the language of the doctrine of the Trinity. This theological language maintains all the truths about the nature of God discussed in the opening chapters of this book, while also encompassing the new revelation about God's inner life opened for us by Christ. To the development of this language and its importance to our faith, we will now turn.

7

Speaking about the Trinity

Having established that the Bible reveals to us a God who is one but who is also Father, Son, and Holy Spirit, how do we speak about this mystery and what bearing does it have on the way we think about God? Christians from the New Testament onward did express the divinity of Christ and the communal life of God in different ways, but in the fourth century the need to develop precise language about the relationship of the Father and Son arose. This honing of theological language was necessary because of a controversy that began in Egypt, originating with a priest named Arius. Arius was worried that speaking of Christ as God, completely equal with the Father, threatened the unique nature of God. He worried, in other words, that the doctrine of the Trinity was irreconcilable with monotheism and so also threatened God's transcendence, his immutability, his omnipotence, and so on. Arius instead proposed that Jesus was the first of all created things, perfect and sinless, but not coequal with God. To resolve this issue, the Church convened the very first ecumenical council, the council of Nicea in 325. It is from this council that we receive the Nicene creed, a version of which is professed at Mass every Sunday. The council, in order to preserve the biblical mystery of Christ's oneness with the Father, denounced Arius's ideas. And, if you stop to think about the words of the creed, you may realize that the section on Christ is much longer than the section on either the Father or the Holy Spirit, and that it carefully lays out the Son's eternal relationship with the Father against Arius's theology:

> I believe in one Lord Jesus Christ,
> the Only Begotten Son of God,
> born of the Father before all ages.
> God from God, Light from Light,
> true God from true God,
> begotten, not made, consubstantial with the Father;
> through him all things were made.[1]

In the creed we have the foundation of the doctrine of the Trinity, that is, the foundation of the Church's way of speaking about God as being three and one. The Word, who became man in Jesus Christ, is the Son of God not in time as if he were born like we are, but he is eternally Son of the Father. Christ is God, he is light, he is *begotten, not made* and *through him all things were made.* By saying that Christ is begotten, the creed expresses the kind of relation the Son has with the Father, which we will discuss further in a moment. Here it suffices to say that the Son's relationship with the Father is not the same as the Father's relationship to creation. The Word is *not made*, unlike a human being, an animal, or even an angel. The distinction between creator and created is reinforced by the last line, which echoes the prologue of John (i.e., Jn 1:2). Through the Word all things were made, and therefore the Word is not himself among created things. Christ is also said to be *consubstantial with the Father.* The word "consubstantial" means that Christ is one in substance, nature, or being with the Father. As we laid out in the first few chapters, God's nature refers to what God is and what he can do. So, in the creed, by professing that Christ is

---

1   "The Nicene Creed." What We Believe, USCCB, http://www.usccb.org/beliefs-and-teachings/.

consubstantial with the Father, we profess that Christ is God and that he is God in every single way that the Father is God. He is the same *what* as God the Father.

These statements in the Nicene creed therefore give us the foundation for understanding how the Father, Son, and Holy Spirit are one. They are one because they all possess the divine nature; they are consubstantial. We know that the divine nature is wholly simple and without parts, and therefore each of the persons of the Trinity is fully and completely God—they do not divide up divinity among themselves. The substance or nature of God is not divine "stuff" out of which the three are made. Nor does each person of the Trinity take up a part or piece of God that when added together makes one whole God. Because God is simple, moreover, we also know that he is what he does and what he has, and so the three are also one in activity and possession. The three persons do not have different jobs or roles nor do they have different characteristics. There is only one God, only one *what*, a simple and entire divine nature.

If God is one in this complete and entire way, however, then how can God be said to be three—the Father, Son, and Holy Spirit? Our biblical evidence showed us that the three were named distinctly and that the Son could pray to the Father as to someone else, and so we have already hinted at the answer to this question. Although God is only one *what*, God is also three *whos*. We make this kind of distinction all the time in our everyday classification of things. We might ask "What is it?" and the answer could be "a cat." A question asked about the same cat—"who is it?"—would be answered differently (perhaps "Fluffy"). Of human beings, we can also understand the difference between nature (the *what* of a human being, the human-ness) and the person (the name, a particular human being). Of course, in the Trinity, the distinction between the persons is not exactly like the one between human beings, because two human beings can never be completely united in action and possession, and two people can never be so unified that they are wholly simple as God is. But, this way of speaking shows us that the distinction between the three persons of the Trinity lies only in the inner relationships within the Godhead, in the identity of the persons. Put otherwise, there is no external measure by which the three can be distinguished, but only by their internal relations to one another. The Son has everything the Father has except his being Father. The Holy Spirit has everything the Son has except his being Son, and so on.

It is for this reason that the Son is called, in the creed, the "only-begotten." The word "begotten" is used of the Son in a number of places in the Bible (primarily in John's Gospel), and it is also chosen by the Fathers of Nicea to describe the relationship of Father and Son that is unique to them. If we recall our discussion of analogous language, we know that we can have some sense of this relationship, because we have some sense of the meaning of the words "Son" and "begotten." We know what it is like to have a child on this earth, and how a mother shares herself with the child whom she begets. We know what it means for parents to love their children even more than themselves, and so to give of themselves. Although the Son perfectly shares the substance of the Father and is also begotten eternally, unlike in the case of human birth, we know by analogy some part of what begetting and sonship mean. For this reason, Paul writes in Ephesians: "I bow my knees before the Father [*patera*], after whom every family [*patria*] in heaven and on earth is named" (Eph 3:15).[2] Or, as Thomas Aquinas would put it, the fatherhood (and motherhood) we name on earth pre-exists in a higher way in God. God is Father by begetting and giving eternally, and of this we have some notion because of human parenthood.

---

2   I have included the Greek transliterations to make clear the analogy of fatherhood Paul is putting forth in this verse.

Likewise, the Holy Spirit is distinguished from Father and Son by his relation to them. The word used to signal the special relationship of the Holy Spirit to the Father and Son also appears in the creed (from a version written a little later, in 381):[3]

I believe in the Holy Spirit,
The Lord, the giver of life
Who proceeds from the Father (and the Son).[4]

The word used for the Holy Spirit's relationality with the Father and Son is "proceeds." Although this word may not have as strong a hold on our imagination as "begotten," a different word must be used to identify the unique place of the Holy Spirit within the Godhead. The word "proceed" is taken from the words of Christ in John 15:26: "But when the Helper comes, whom I will send to you from the Father, the Spirit of truth, who proceeds from the Father, he will bear witness about me." The word "spiration" is sometimes used as well, drawing on the imagery of the Holy Spirit as the breath of life and the exhaling of the life of God to us.

We have now laid out the language that the Church uses to proclaim both the unity and plurality of God. God is one in nature, substance, or being. There is only one God who is infinite, eternal, and the like. But God is three in his inner life; there are three persons—the Father, Son, and Holy Spirit—who exist eternally in communion with one another,

---

3   The creed professed in the liturgy is not the creed of 325, but a revised version from the second ecumenical council of Constantinople in 381. The object of this revision was to include a fuller statement on the Holy Spirit, as the council of 325 was mostly concerned with Arius's teachings on the Son.

4   The phrase "and the Son" (Latin: *filioque*) does not appear in the creed of 381, but began to be professed in some places in the West around a hundred years later, and it is also in our modern version of the creed in the West. It is beyond the scope of this book to discuss why this phrase was added and the significance attached to it, but it remains an issue of contention between the Western and Eastern churches. For further reading on this issue, see a brief treatment in *CCC*, 246–48. For a longer treatment, see Aidan Nichols, *Rome and the Eastern Churches* (San Francisco: Ignatius Press, 1992), 227–71 (chap. 7).

distinguished only by their relations. The word "person" is used here to designate the three rather than "people" or "aspects" or any other word. Although no word can ever perfectly describe God, this word "person" is chosen to indicate distinction without separation. The three cannot be divided or pulled apart, and so they are not three people. But they are also truly distinct, not just aspects or perspectives of the same thing.

Another way to think about how this oneness and threeness functions is to meditate on the inner life of God as pure activity, a concept we have already encountered. If God is activity, then his inner life is not one of stagnation or boredom. He is not a monolith suspended outside time and space, but he somehow acts eternally without changing. Let us consider for a moment the possibility of God thinking about himself. God knows all things, including himself. He is simple and complete. His thought about himself, therefore, cannot be anything other than an entire and complete self-knowledge that is lacking in nothing, and yet one's thought about oneself is not identical with the one thinking. The biblical imagery used of the Son encourages us to contemplate his relation to the Father in this way, that is, as the Father's perfect self-representation. The Son is called by Paul "the image of the invisible God" (Col 1:15), not merely "in/after the image" (Gn 1:26), like we are. Christ is the full and complete reflection of God the Father. Hebrews describes the same idea in the following way, saying that the Son "is the radiance of the glory of God and the exact imprint of his nature, and he upholds the universe by the word of his power" (Heb 1:3). Even we as human beings possess our own identity by knowledge of ourselves. If we forget who we are, we cannot act fully as ourselves. In God, this self-knowledge is perfect and complete. It is a person. It is his Word, Image, Power, and Wisdom (cf. 1 Cor 1:24). Likewise, we might consider how God loves himself, especially in light of 1 John, which tells us that "God is love" (1 Jn 4:8). God's love of himself would be in full knowledge of himself and could be nothing other than a full outpouring of himself (not like our self-love, which can be deluded, prideful, and distorted). Thus, it too is a person who proceeds from Father and Son: the Holy Spirit.

Reflecting on our understanding of the unity and plurality of God, we can see how God is three-in-one, not because three equals one in some impossible math equation, but because God is three persons in one nature, and their unity is constituted by their perfect relationship with one another. That God is three therefore undergirds a true understanding of God's unity, because it is not a unity that is flat or static, a unity—we might say—of homogeneity, but rather a unity of perfect communion and relationality. It is a unity of substance but also a unity of persons. The persons are not only related to one another, as in a family with father, mother, aunts, and uncles, but they are always fully given to one another. The theological term to describe the resting of the persons of the Trinity in one another is "circumincession." Another word for this inner activity-in-harmony is "perichoresis," a Greek word that is related to the English word "choreography." The concept of perichoresis images the Trinity as an eternal dance, an indwelling, a flowing from-and-to, an exchange.

We come now to the question of how these theological formulations, built on scriptural meditation, affect our everyday Christian life. Coming up for air from all of these precise distinctions, we might be tempted to think that the doctrine of the Trinity is best left to theologians, and that we have now gone quite far enough. But, of course, we did set out in this book determined to understand God more deeply so that we may love him better, and God's innermost life revealed to us in Christ is the most precious revelation he has given to us because it is the hidden knowledge of his very own self. God, in fact, so desires that we learn about his own inner life—to which we would have no access by external observation, given that the Trinity is unified in action—that the persons of the Trinity do indeed act in distinct ways from our perspective within history in order for us to have some sense of who they are. For example, we can see that the mission of the Son and the Holy Spirit in the world corresponds to some degree to the inner life of the Trinity. The Son is the one who comes to earth as Jesus Christ and preaches to us, and whose words and life constitute the Gospels, a fitting mission for the one who is the Word. We also often speak of Christ as the savior. Calling Christ our savior, however, does not mean that he saves us without the Father and the Holy Spirit. After all, we would not want to say that the Father and Holy Spirit do *not* save us. However, assigning a role to the Son helps us see in some small way how he is the only-begotten and how he can be offered as a sacrifice to the Father. The Holy Spirit, likewise, as the one who proceeds from Father and Son in love is also the one who is spoken of as dwelling in our hearts and enabling us to love and to pray to God. In his letter to the Romans, Paul writes, "[Y]ou have received the Spirit of adoption as sons, by whom we cry, 'Abba! Father!'" (Rom 8:15). Again, speaking of the Spirit as the one who is received within us does not mean that we do *not* have Christ and God the Father also in our hearts, but speaking of the Spirit in this way helps us see in some small degree the life of the Spirit within the Godhead. God reveals himself to us in this way through his work in the world that we might come to know him. The term used for assigning roles within salvation history to the persons of the Trinity is called "the doctrine of appropriation," because actions within time are appropriated to each of the three persons. Therefore, by external and visible action, the Trinity shares itself with our human intellects and, as Frank Sheed writes, "It is the surest mark of love to want to be known."[5] For this reason, God shares the knowledge of his own inner life; God loves us. It is his love that we shrug off when we treat the doctrine of the Trinity as just so many confusing words. We should be persistent in our contemplation of the Trinity, therefore, because, as Aquinas puts it, it is "the perfect knowledge of God in which consists eternal bliss."[6] Aquinas does not mean by this that heaven will be like a university, or an endless theology book (heaven forbid!), but that it will be perfect intimacy with God and with each other. We will know and be known.

Since God so wants to communicate his inner life with us, and the doctrine of the Trinity is essential to coming to know God better, it should come as no surprise that the doctrine of the Trinity also has many immediate applications to other mysteries of the Christian faith. Knowing this doctrine should, in the first instance, give us new perspective when reading the Scriptures. It should make us attentive to the actions appropriated to Son and Spirit in the Bible so that we may know them more intimately. It should bring us new insights on the progressive revelation of God's character in the Old Testament. The doctrine of the Trinity also has profound implications for contemplating Christian unity. This idea was already apparent in the passages from John's Gospel when Jesus was speaking about his unity with the Father. When we understand more of the Trinity, we understand more about the unity to which God calls his Church and the whole human race. We are to be one as the Father and Son are one, not to compete with one another, but to give our whole selves over fully to those to whom we are united. This Trinitarian character of Christian unity also means that we should never grow lazy in striving for the unification of all

---

5   Frank Sheed, *Theology and Sanity* (San Francisco: Ignatius Press, 1993), 90.
6   Aquinas, *Summa Theologiae* Ia, q. 1, a. 4.

Christians, because Christ desires us to have the deepest form of unity possible with one another. When we speak therefore of the Church as "the body of Christ" (cf. 1 Cor 2:12–27; Eph 4:1–16), we are not merely using a metaphor, but we are speaking of the Church as our means of unity with the Godhead, that is, our inauguration into the life of the Trinity. In baptism, we become one with Christ who is one with the Father, and so through his body we come into communion with the Trinity. We are also speaking about the sharing of all things (spiritual and material) with our brothers and sisters. In sum, we cannot understand what the Church is and what it is meant to be without the doctrine of the Trinity.

The doctrine of the Trinity also gives us a new appreciation and understanding of creation, as John demonstrates in the opening of his Gospel. We have already laid out above that God creates from no need or lack of his own because he is perfect. But, knowing the doctrine of the Trinity, we also know that God's perfection consists of complete relationality and love. God does not create because he is lonely, or because he lacks some companionship that creatures are going to provide. God is a perfect communion of love in himself. Therefore, in creation, what God bestows on us is his very own life of love. The doctrine of the Trinity teaches us that God himself is the love that he gives.

8

Analogies for the Trinity

We have now laid out the formal theological language the Church uses to describe the doctrine of the Trinity, and some broader implications of this teaching, but are there any other ways to explain this doctrine and come to understand it better? In popular preaching and teaching on the Trinity, analogies tend to be used quite frequently. This practice is not wrong in and of itself, as we have learned, since we come to know God by analogy with things in creation. Nevertheless, the use of analogies is only helpful if they can propel us forward in our understanding of the mystery to which they are referring, and not if the analogy serves as an intellectual crutch that essentially replaces the thing for which it is supposed to be only an analogy. In other words, analogies are good so long as we are aware that they are analogies. One way to remind ourselves of the proper use of analogies is to point out the shortcomings of any analogy we come across. In this way, both the positive and negative way of ascending to knowledge of God can be united. An analogy about God can give us a hint of divine things, but remembering the limitations of that analogy can remind us what God is not and that no analogy can ever fully capture the mystery of the Trinity. In this chapter, we will first consider some Trinitarian analogies that have more shortcomings than strengths, and then step-by-step proceed to consider some analogies that can be a little more useful in coming to a deeper understanding of the Trinity. We will end with a brief consideration of the Trinity in actual images—that is, the Trinity in art.

Perhaps one of the first Trinitarian images that comes to mind is a three-leafed clover or fleur-de-lis. The analogy, purportedly used by St. Patrick to explain the Trinity, is used as an example of something that is one and also three: there is only one clover, but it has three leaves. Although we sometimes use very simple analogies to get a basic point across (in this case, how something could be three and also one), as St. Patrick might have done when evangelizing a nation completely unfamiliar with the Christian faith, this analogy can introduce lazy thinking about the Trinity. The three-leafed clover is not really three-in-one, but it is one thing with three parts. Although the three share a substance (i.e., the clover-ness), the substance is divided into three equal parts, and if you plucked off one of the leaves, the clover would be diminished. The clover therefore does not represent the unity that the Trinity possesses. The Trinity is not one third Father, one third Son, one third Holy Spirit, but each possess the divine nature entirely and undividedly. Nor could one be plucked out from the others, since they dwell and rest in one another. Likewise, the three leaves of the clover are essentially interchangeable, with one being basically a copy of the other. The clover, therefore, does not represent the distinction of the persons either, since there is no difference in relation and no ordering within the three leaves. Although images of the three-leafed clover can serve as visual reminders or symbols of our Trinitarian faith, they are not particularly useful in contemplating the mystery of unity-in-diversity as it exists in the Trinity. A similar analogy, but even less useful, is that of an egg (the yolk, the white, and the shell in one egg). This analogy is once again something with three parts that creates one whole, but in this case the three parts are not even made of the same "stuff," but can be clearly distinguished by their composition.

Another analogy with a slightly different approach is the analogy to the states of water. The analogy is as follows: as water can be ice, liquid, or steam, but still has the same chemical composition in each state (analogous to substance), so Father, Son, and Holy Spirit share a substance but have distinct expressions of that substance. It may be less immediately apparent why this analogy is wide of the mark, but it is an analogy that lends itself to a Trinitarian error called "Sabellianism" or "modalism." This way of thinking about the Trinity sees God as a monad who only expresses himself differently in different situations (i.e., one God with different modes). The distinction between liquid water, ice, and steam, in other words, is not an internal or relational difference. The distinction is not like that of unbegotten and begotten (for instance), but it is only a difference of manifestation based on external circumstances (in this case, the temperature of the water). The distinction amongst the persons of the Trinity is quite the opposite; it is a distinction only of internal life, not of external perception, and it is not brought about by outside pressures. Similar to this analogy is that of a man who is a husband, a father, and a fireman all at the same time. Once again, this distinction is one only of the man's *roles*, not of three unified persons in one substance. A man is a husband from the perspective of his wife, an outside observer. This distinction is not one that exists within his very being, but it is a role that could change with circumstances. It is also not an identity that he has always had. In the case of the Trinity, however, the different roles (e.g., in salvation) are an external expression of an inner relation of persons that is for the benefit of our understanding, but the relational distinctions themselves are eternal and unchanging.

Another image that has gained widespread popularity, especially in light of St. John Paul II's *Theology of the Body*, is the image of the human family.[1] Here, we need to make an important distinction. We have already introduced the idea that in human relationships and in human parentage we can see an analogy of the Father's relationship to the Son. We have also suggested that we are meant for communion with each other just as the Father, Son, and Holy Spirit are a communion. These propositions remain true. Nevertheless, seeing the human family as an analogy for the Trinity in the way that it is sometimes proposed is highly problematic. First comes the question of which person of the Trinity is which for the analogy in question. Clearly the Father would be equated with the human father, but is the "mother" to be understood as the Son because the Holy Spirit proceeds from Father and Son in love, as children are conceived by their parents? If so, we would have a rather perplexing situation where the Son (the second person of the Trinity) is the "mother" in the analogy and the Holy Spirit is the "son" or "child," even though in the language of the Trinity it is the Son who is begotten of the Father. If we change the analogy and have the Holy Spirit be the "mother," then we would seem to reverse the order of relation in the Trinity (to an ordering of Father, Holy Spirit, Son), as well as the order of the unveiling of the persons of the Trinity in salvation history, where the Spirit is given last to dwell in our hearts. Perhaps an even more significant problem is that this analogy images the persons of the Trinity as simply being three people, and three people who are unequal at that (given that children are subordinate to their parents, and subsequent to them in time). Although three people have a common human nature, they are clearly able to be separated and divided. The three people would have a different appearance, age, and so on. They possess many

---

1   John Paul II himself did not misuse this analogy so much as adaptations of his work have sometimes done so. He asserts in many places that the image of God is found in our intellectual nature, such as the example discussed in chapter 10.

external markers by which they could be distinguished. The Trinity, simply put, is not the same as three people who love one another.

Added to this problem of conceptualizing the family analogy when it comes down to the particulars is the fact that this analogy can tend to elevate marriage beyond all other human vocations. If we see in a marriage with children the primary image of the Trinity, this seems to exclude many people—including those in religious life—from imaging the Trinity in the highest way. It is for this reason that Augustine rejected the analogy of the family as suitable, because it obscures the fact that each human being is made in the image of God, not three people put together.[2] The love of the Trinity has, of course, left its imprint on the structure of the human family, and from the family we can learn about intra-trinitarian love, but we should not hasten to use the family as the principal analogy for explaining the concept of three persons with one nature. In using this analogy, we are particularly prone to reduce the Trinity to human terms and to stop pressing further in our understanding of God.

Augustine proposes a different analogy, which is not so unlike the analogy of the human family, and yet it is not that of three people loving one another *per se*, but one based on the Trinitarian nature of love itself, wherever love is to be found. Augustine takes his cue from 1 John 4:8 ("God is love"), from which we have already drawn some of our own reflections on the Trinity. Augustine reasons that when you consider love in and of itself, you will find that it is inherently three. One cannot love in the abstract; we must love someone or something. So, Augustine says, we find that where love is, there are three: the lover (the one who loves), the beloved (the

---

2   See Augustine, *On the Trinity*, trans. Edmund Hill (Hyde Park, N.Y.: New City Press, 2007), 12.2.

one who is loved, the object), and the love itself. The persons of the Trinity correspond to these three as they proceed in the Godhead: the lover is Father, the beloved is the Son, and the love is the Holy Spirit.

In this analogy of Augustine's, we can come to some deeper considerations of the unity of the Trinity. First, the three in the analogy cannot exist in isolation. You cannot "pluck" one from the other, as in the clover analogy. Without a beloved, there can be no such thing as a lover, and without love, neither beloved nor lover could exist. Therefore, the idea of an inseparable and indivisible unity is maintained by this analogy. There is a certain ordering within the three, as the lover must love first, but, there is also simultaneity of the three, since love and beloved exist as soon as the lover begins loving. This analogy serves as an approximation for eternally begetting within the Trinity, where there is an ordering (the Father is the unbegotten and first principle), and yet there is also simultaneity, since the Son is begotten and the Spirit proceeds eternally, as soon as the Father loves (which is always). Second, the distinction between the three in the analogy is based on internal relations. The lover is defined as such because of the beloved, and their love is constituted by their relationship to one another. The inner working of this love could be told to others, but its distinctions rest within the relationship. So it is with God, who communicates his love to us in human language, but his identity does not depend on us. Third, there is a sharing of "substance," one might say, a sharing of love, but there really is nothing else other than love in the analogy. Such is the case also with God, who "shares" his substance among three, and yet he is also identical with his substance. When using this analogy, therefore, we are not likely to make the mistake of thinking that substance or nature is some kind of stuff divided up into three parts. Rather, it is a wholly shared nature. The analogy also draws from the biblical understanding of God as love, and the Son as beloved of the Father (as at Jesus's baptism, cited above: "This is my beloved Son, with whom I am well pleased").

But perhaps the most compelling part of this analogy is that it is not one of three people in love exactly, but one of love itself as having an inherent three-ness. This aspect of the analogy helps us to understand God because God is not merely a Trinity of persons who have a communion amongst themselves; rather, the three persons *are* a communion of love. Likewise, in the analogy, it is love itself that is the expression and bond of the lover and beloved. Similarly, God's love, the Holy Spirit, is a person. Augustine, for this reason, also calls the Holy Spirit a gift, because God's love has its own proper existence such that we can pray to the Holy Spirit and the Holy Spirit can be given to us. But, the weakness of this analogy that is most often pointed out is in this role of the Holy Spirit. It could seem that the third person—love—does not quite have a personal character as do the lover and beloved, and we can hardly imagine what it would be like to have love so real that it itself can be counted as a third. But maybe in this dissimilarity to human experience (since our love does not have this kind of existence) we can strive to see also how God's love differs from ours.

Augustine himself felt the analogy of love ultimately fell short of what he wanted to express about the Trinity, and so he developed a further analogy, which he believed came closer. He especially wanted to find an analogy that reflected the truth that each person is made in the image of God, and that the image is to be found daily at work in us. He found such an analogy in the intellectual operations of the human person: in our memory, understanding, and will. To demonstrate this analogy, consider an action that we do all the time: speaking. When we are speaking, we must remember the words, we must understand their meaning, and we must perform the actual act of verbalizing those words (whether those words are spoken internally to ourselves or out loud to other people). We can see in these three actions an ordering: we could not understand a word without first remembering it and we could not speak coherently without both remembering and understanding. And yet, these three actions happen, even in a human person, virtually simultaneously and interdependently. Here Augustine finds his image: Father (memory), Son (understanding), and Holy Spirit (will/love). Like the Trinity, these three are ordered, and yet there is a perfect sharing of activity. In this image we also have a unity-in-distinction that comes close to being free of associations of physical division and sharing, and free from the notion of multiple people. The most common critique of Augustine's analogy, however, is that it loses the sense of the persons as a communion of love, although Augustine contended that we only image God when these three are directed toward God—that is, when we remember, understand, and love God. Only then does our mind operate for the purpose that it was intended and thus bear the true image of the Trinity. It is Augustine's desire to know God and to image him that leads him to this final analogy, as is evident from the prayer he writes near the ending of his great work *On the Trinity*:

> O Lord my God, my one hope, listen to me lest out of weariness I should stop wanting to seek you, but let me seek your face always and with ardor. Do you yourself give me the strength to seek, having caused yourself to be found and having given me hope of finding you more and more . . . *Let me remember you, let me understand you, let me love you.* Increase these things in me until you refashion me entirely.[3]

---

3   Ibid., 5.51 (emphasis added).

We can see how Augustine's analogy is therefore indebted to and intertwined with his life of prayer. He comes at the doctrine of the Trinity not with a hammer to crack open its meaning, but on his knees in longing after God. When he remembers, understands, and loves God, only then can he begin to see the Trinity more clearly.

Another analogy that derives from a more mystical tradition comes from St. Ignatius of Loyola (founder of the Society of Jesus). To his biographer, he describes a vision—or rather an audition—that he experienced of the Trinity:

> One day, he was saying the hours of Our Lady on the monastery's steps, his understanding was raised on high, so as to see the Most Holy Trinity under the aspect of three keys on a musical instrument, and as a result he shed many tears and sobbed so strongly he could not control himself.[4]

Ignatius hears the Trinity as a musical chord of three notes, a chord so beautiful that it moves him to tears. The analogy of a chord has a number of strengths to help us further our knowledge of the Trinity. A chord is three notes that are in harmony and yet have a specific progression. The three notes are distinguished precisely by their proper relations to one another, that is, the pitch. A chord also possesses a kind of unity that is not bodily. Nevertheless, there a few weaknesses in this analogy as well: the three notes in a chord can be divided (played separately), unlike the persons of the Trinity, and each note does not possess the entire chord, unlike in the Trinity where each of the three possess the entire divine nature. The strongest part of the analogy, however, is that it captures the idea that in the triune God there is a perfection of beauty that God

---

4   Ignatius of Loyola, *A Pilgrim's Journey,* trans. Joseph Tylenda (San Francisco: Ignatius Press, 2001), 75.

wishes to communicate to us through the senses. The Trinity is a mystery that should make our heart swell at its glory, and not merely make our head hurt. Ignatius's experience of the triune God and Augustine's prayer never to tire of seeking after God can serve to remind us of the beauty of God's self-disclosure, that "God has revealed his innermost secret: God himself is an eternal exchange of love, Father, Son and Holy Spirit, and he has destined us to share in that exchange."[5]

When speaking of analogies or images of the Trinity, there is one topic worthy of discussion before we move on: the depiction of the Trinity in art. Portraying the Trinity in art presents a particular challenge, because unlike Christ and his saints, the Father and Holy Spirit are incorporeal. They are not, in essence, visible. There have been many attempts to resolve this problem so that we can create appropriate aids for contemplating the triune God. Sometimes the Trinity is depicted symbolically, as three interlocking rings, or as a triangle, to name two examples. Such symbolic imagery can certainly remind us of our Trinitarian faith and evoke the triune God, but they do not do much to express things like unity-in-diversity or exchange of love, as our analogies do. These signs and symbols remain simply an echo or evocation of a deeper truth. Although they are surely appropriate in Christian decoration, they are not heavily invested with doctrinal meaning. Other images draw on Trinitarian scenes from the biblical text, such as the baptism of Jesus. The most famous of these is Andrei Rublev's icon of the Trinity, which is a depiction of the three angels who appear to Abraham in Genesis 18. The opening of that story reads as follows:

> And the LORD appeared to him by the oaks of Mamre, as he sat
> at the door of his tent in the heat of the day. He lifted up his

---

5　*CCC*, 221.

eyes and looked, and behold, three men were standing in front of him. When he saw them, he ran from the tent door to meet them and bowed himself to the earth and said, "O LORD, if I have found favor in your sight, do not pass by your servant. Let a little water be brought, and wash your feet, and rest yourselves under the tree, while I bring a morsel of bread, that you may refresh yourselves, and after that you may pass on—since you have come to your servant." (Gn 18:1–5)

Interpreters have often seen in this story an Old Testament hinting or foreshadowing of the Trinity. There are three visitors who come bearing a divine message, and yet Abraham addresses them as a single Lord. Such an image can help us "see" the Trinity, in the sense that it visually depicts a starting point from the biblical text for understanding God and his triune character. In the Rublev icon, the doctrine of the Trinity is further evoked because the three share identical faces but wear different colored clothing, representing the shared nature of three distinct persons. The three also gaze at one another in turn, giving a visual approximation of the three persons who share completely in love and knowledge. One of the figures also gestures at a small dish holding the morsel of bread mentioned in the passage, reminiscent of the Eucharist, an invitation into the communion.

But perhaps the most common images of the Trinity in Western art are those of an old man (God the Father, sometimes depicted as a king, pope, or even high priest), along with Jesus, and a bird (the dove, the form in which the Holy Spirit appeared at Jesus's baptism). Sometimes the Father is holding the Son on the cross, with the Holy Spirit hovering in between them. Other times, the Father and Son are enthroned with the dove between the two. At first glance, these images can seem crude, and even counterproductive for our quest to come to a deeper appreciation of the Trinity. We have expended considerable effort in this book banishing the notion of God as an old man and the Trinity as three people (let alone two people and a bird). In our modern theological climate, these images can indeed be a hindrance to people who do not have a firm grasp of the doctrine of the Trinity, as it is tempting to substitute these images for the true mystery of the Trinity. Nevertheless, we should not understand the artists and commissioners of these paintings to be simply bad theologians who love a pretty picture more than the difficult but sublime doctrine of the Trinity. These images are often carefully trying to translate certain aspects of the doctrine into an emotionally moving visual form. The depiction of God as an old man, especially when he is holding the crucified Christ, reminds us of his fatherly love and care, which we can understand from his appearance as older than the Son, and often from his facial expression. The Father and Son frequently share a similar or identical face, moreover, to show the kind of essential unity that Rublev was aiming at, a kind of familial likeness. The position of the Holy Spirit is also meant to communicate the bond of love between Father and Son. These images, on the whole, are inspired by the doctrine of appropriation, where we can see the action of the Trinity in history as reflective of the truth of the Trinity's inner life: Father as originator and creator, Son as redeemer, Holy Spirit as sanctifier—the one sent into our hearts. The majority of these images show a moment in salvation history, but, from a heavenly viewpoint, most often Christ's sacrifice on the cross, and so the image is necessarily an appropriation. If such images can give to us a deeper sense of the love of the Trinity and the extension of that love to us, then they can serve a useful intellectual and devotional function.

9

The Trinity Is the Central
Mystery of Christian Life

Now that we have spent some time contemplating the mystery of the Trinity, we can return to a statement made in the *Catechism* that appeared in the introduction of this book, namely, that the doctrine of the Trinity is the central mystery of Christian faith *and* life.[1] This statement is not just paying lip service to the doctrine of the Trinity. Let us not pass it over. The *Catechism* is telling us that the Trinity is not only the end goal of our faith and of our contemplation because it is the mystery of God, that it is not only something we should spend time thinking about, but the doctrine of the Trinity should also be the beginning and end of our Christian life and our activity. We now know that the doctrine of the Trinity is central because it is God revealing himself so that we may come to know and love him, and that the very revelation of God's inner-trinitarian life is also our invitation into it (e.g., in the Gospel of John and at Jesus's baptism). We also have already discussed many of the theological implications of this doctrine (some examples we gave were biblical study, Christian unity, and creation). But how does this centrality of the Trinity look day to day, in the practice of our faith and in our striving for virtue?

---

1   See *CCC*, 234.

One simple way in which we might recognize how our Christian lives are marked by the doctrine of the Trinity is in our daily practice of making the sign of the cross. When we make this outward sign, we inscribe on our bodies the Christian faith in sum. In this gesture, we proclaim faith in the Father, the Son, and the Holy Spirit, as well as faith in our salvation by the wood of the cross. This ritual that, for most Catholics, is completely commonplace joins the Christian faith and the Christian life every time we make it, because the sign of the cross is not just shorthand for a theological teaching, but it is a prayer, a sign of blessing and an act of reverence before God. We therefore are not just teaching the fact of the doctrine of the Trinity (that God is three-in-one) when we make the sign of the cross, but we are praying to God who is Trinity, we are blessing in the name of the God who is Trinity, and we are worshipping the God who is Trinity. The doctrine of the Trinity shapes our worship in a real and tangible way because we mark our bodies with the sign of the triune God every day. It is particularly fitting that this act should be so outward and visible, because it reflects what God has revealed to us outwardly, and it also signals the fact that we, as regular human beings with regular human bodies, can hope to share in the Trinity's life. It shows the intimacy we have with God, and that we hope to have in heaven, because God has revealed himself to us. As we should never grow weary of searching for God, let us never grow weary of making the sign of the cross, by which we may physically and ritually proclaim ourselves to belong to God, and to give ourselves ever more to the love that God is. Augustine calls the sign of the cross "a sign more precious than any jewel,"[2] because when we wear this sign it shows forth the invisible mark of our

---

2   Augustine, *Expositions of the Psalms*, trans. Maria Boulding, vol. 1 (Hyde Park, N.Y.: New City Press, 2000), 32.3.13.

baptism, and so is a more beautiful adornment than anything else we could obtain.

There are also many other moments in the liturgy that are shaped by the doctrine of the Trinity and proclaim it. The Trinity, of course, is invoked many times explicitly (e.g., "in the name of the Father, and of the Son, and of the Holy Spirit"), but there also other subtler ways in which our worship is caught up into the mystery of the Trinity. Perhaps one of the most poignant is the hymn of the angels, the *Sanctus* ("Holy, Holy, Holy, Lord God of Hosts . . ."), sung in the Mass shortly before the consecration of the bread and wine. The hymn, based on Isaiah 6:3, is given new meaning for us by the version found in the book of Revelation:

> And the four living creatures, each of them with six wings,
> are full of eyes all around and within, and day and night
> they never cease to say,
>   "Holy, holy, holy, is the Lord God Almighty,
>   who was and is and is to come!" (Rev 4:8)

Here the author of Revelation is seeing a vision of heaven and of the worship happening before the throne of God. Both the angels and the saints are casting down their crowns and singing praises to God as Trinity, the thrice-holy, who is described as being eternal but in a threefold way (he was, and is, and is to come). When we sing the *Sanctus*, we are experiencing a foretaste of the worship of heaven, which is eternal communion with the Trinity, the thrice-holy one. The mystery of the Trinity stands at the heart of the Mass, where we receive the body of Christ in order to come into communion with God, that is, with the Trinity. The Eucharist is a source of grace not because it is a spiritual superfood, but because by it we truly receive the life of the Trinity and we are prepared ever more fully by it for the communion with God that we hope to have in heaven. Or, as the *Catechism* puts it, "The Eucharist is the efficacious sign and sublime cause of *that communion in the divine life and that unity of the People of God* by which the Church is kept in being."[3] In other words, the Eucharist is communion with God and with each other, not as a sign only but in fact (the "sublime cause" of communion). The Trinity, therefore, is not just the most important abstract concept for us to contemplate amongst the things in the faith we could contemplate, but it is also the mystery in which we participate at Mass, and the mystery we proclaim with our voices and the liturgical actions of our body. The Eucharist initiates us into the divine life and unites us to one another because it is the sacramental sharing of God's own triune life.

As the doctrine of the Trinity shapes our liturgical practice, so also it shapes the way we pray and can give us a renewed sense of the intimacy with God that we experience in prayer. Although there are prayers addressed to each of the persons of the Trinity, by the doctrine of appropriation, prayer is often described as *to* the Father, *with* the Son and *in/by* the Holy Spirit. A good verse to begin thinking about this is Romans 8:15, which we have already discussed briefly: "For you did not receive the spirit of slavery to fall back into fear, but you have received the Spirit of adoption as sons, by whom we cry, 'Abba! Father!'" Following Paul, our prayers are often addressed to the first person of the Trinity, God the Father, to whom we tend to associate the idea of complete transcendence, creation, and omnipotence. The Father is the one who may seem the most distant. But we do not call on God as servants or subjects, but rather, as sons, as children of God. The reason that we can call out to God as sons is because of the Son, who became man and enabled us to be adopted by God in baptism. We can have a baptism like Christ's to share in his sonship,

---

3   *CCC*, 1325 (emphasis added).

and therefore with him pray to God as Father. So, we pray to God (the Father) because of God coming among us (the Son), but we also pray by God dwelling in our hearts (the Holy Spirit). We are enabled to pray to God by God's indwelling. In this way, an acknowledgment of God's transcendence and immanence is united in every act of prayer. We call out to the God who is far above (Father) because of the God who came near to us (Son) by the God who dwells within us now (Holy Spirit)—the God who is three and one, the God who is both transcendent and immanent. When we pray, therefore, we do so to the Trinity and by the Trinity; this doctrine is always alongside us.

If the examples above have given some indication of how the doctrine of the Trinity shapes and informs the spiritual life, what about the moral life? Can we see how God's innermost life has a bearing on the way that we act? The perfection of the moral life—living as we ought—is charity, the greatest of all virtues. As Paul says: "For now we see in a mirror dimly, but then face to face. Now I know in part; then I shall know fully, even as I have been fully known. So now faith, hope, and love abide, these three; but the greatest of these is love" (1 Cor 13:12–13). Paul indelibly links knowing God, being known by God, and the highest end of love, so even in his words we know that faith and life are unified. But it also indicates to us what we are pursuing when we pursue charity. We are not pursuing this or that good action, but we are pursuing God himself, because he is love, indeed, an eternal exchange of love. To know how to act and to act rightly is to pursue unity with God and to imitate the unity that he himself is. We must learn to rest continually in others and give to others, the exchange that defines God's inner life. When we spoke in chapter 7 about the Trinity as the basis of Christian unity, therefore, this was not just true mystically or theoretically speaking, but also practically speaking. We seek to imitate the full self-gift of the Trinity in our attitude toward others. We seek unity of action and purpose. We seek to hold nothing back but to give of ourselves all we can give. When we see another person experiencing goodness, that goodness is also for us, and we can rejoice with them. When we see another person suffer, we suffer with them, and we can mourn with them. This sharing of joy and sorrow should be especially true of those in the Church, since we are part of Christ's mystical body through baptism and have the life of the Trinity at work in us. And, what we give in love we know will be returned to us in full from the God who gives himself without being diminished. In Catherine Doherty's "Little Mandate," Doherty coined this little Trinitarian moral code that just about sums it up: "Love, love, love never counting the cost."[4]

---

4   For the whole text of the mandate and more information on Doherty's writings, see Robert Wild, *Journey to the Heart of Christ: The Little Mandate of God to Catherine Doherty* (Ogdensburg, N.Y.: Madonna House Publications, 2002).

10

The Meaning of "Made in the Image of God"

Having now become familiar with what we can know about the nature of God and what the Bible teaches us about God's Trinitarian life, we can consider an intimately related question: if we now know something about who God is, what does it mean for humankind to be made "in the image of God"? We have already seen that, for St. Augustine, the search for analogies or images for the Trinity was impossible without looking also within the human person, because the Bible tells us that we ought to find the image of God there. Indeed, as mentioned earlier, it is in a passage that evokes the triune God (where God is speaking in the first-person plural) that we find the reference to humankind being made in God's image:

> Then God said, "Let us make man in our image, after our likeness. And let them have dominion over the fish of the sea and over the birds of the heavens and over the livestock and over all the earth and over every creeping thing that creeps on the earth." (Gn 1:26)

This passage tells us that God reserved a special dignity for humankind above all the animals and that this dignity was a share in something God himself is. But what kind of likeness can we have to God, especially considering that God is three persons in one nature (which we are not), and that he is infinite and omnipotent (which we are not)?

Thomas Aquinas, following the Christian tradition, answers that the image of God in human beings "chiefly consists" in our "intellectual nature."[1] Although all things in existence share some likeness to God, due to the fact that they exist and God is the highest existence, we image God especially because of our reason. This idea is suggested also by the book of Genesis, because human beings are placed over the animals and Adam even names the animals (cf. Gn 2:19). It is also Adam's and Eve's ability to reason and make their own decisions that leads to the Fall in Genesis 3, where knowledge is tied to Godlikeness (cf. Gn 3:5, 22). In short, we are rational creatures. We can think, discern, and will to act, and so we can create and love—all of the things that God does perfectly. Aquinas's understanding of how we image God is related to Augustine's analogy for the Trinity as that of the human mind, since Augustine also saw in the inner workings of our reason an echo or pattern of the divine.

But saying that we image God because of our intellect is not meant to imply that smarter people image God better, or that God created us to be a race of academics. The human intellect images God because it is the intellect that is capable of knowing God and therefore of loving him. Without the freedom vouchsafed by the image of God in us, without our ability to think and choose, we cannot offer ourselves to God as free creatures. For this reason, Augustine is fascinated by human memory, which holds together all our experiences and stores even our memories of God deep within ourselves (and so he includes memory as the first principle of his Trinitarian image). In this way, God can be known intimately by us because knowledge of him can reside within us. Augustine writes,

---

1   *Summa Theologiae* I, q. 93, a. 3.

behold, how far within my memory have I travelled in search of you Lord, and beyond it I have not found you . . . For since I learned of you, I have not forgotten you. Wheresoever I found truth, there I found my God, truth itself, and since I first learned the truth I have not forgotten it. Therefore, ever since I learned about you, you abide in my memory and I find you there when I recall you to mind and take delight in you.[2]

If our final beatitude consists in knowing God wholly and completely (or, to use Augustine's categories, by receiving God in our inmost memory, that we might apprehend and love him), it is the intellect that allows us to obtain this bliss. Being made in the image of God, therefore, does not mean only that we are made for the capacity to do difficult math problems (or to read theology books!). It means that we are created capable of sharing God's very life. We are like God because we can—like God—become participants in the life of the Trinity, which is an external exchange of knowing and loving. St. Athanasius puts it this way: "[T]hrough this gift of Godlikeness in themselves they may be able to perceive the Image Absolute, that is the Word Himself, and through Him to apprehend the Father; which knowledge of their Maker is for men the only really happy and blessed life."[3]

A further distinction is sometimes, in the Christian theological tradition, made between the word "image" and the word "likeness," although in the text of Genesis itself these words are likely more or less synonymous. Nevertheless, this distinction can help us understand how we still bear within us the imprint of God, even though we are inhibited by sin in a way that Adam and Eve were not. We *image* God by our intellectual nature, but we are only truly *like* God when we

---

2   *Confessions*, 10.24.35.
3   Athanasius, *On the Incarnation*, trans. Penelope Lawson (Crestwood, N.Y.: St. Vladimir's Seminary Press, 1996), 11.

fully participate in his inner life and share his glory. So while human beings were made in both the image and the likeness (i.e., with intellects and wills that were in a harmonious relationship with God), we currently possess the image while striving ever more to regain the likeness. Aquinas says that the two words (image and likeness) are not fundamentally different in meaning, but we can take likeness to refer to the perfection of the image.[4] Or, to speak in a more Augustinian way, we bear the image of God because of our intellectual nature (our memory, understanding, and will), but it is only when these faculties are the cause of our union with God that we can be said truly to image the Trinity.

What becomes, then, of the idea that our interpersonal relationships also somehow mirror the life of the Trinity? St. John Paul II says that "man became the image of God not only through his own humanity, but also through the communion of persons which man and woman form from the very beginning."[5] He says, in other words, that we are made in the image of God individually, but we are also made male and female in Genesis 1:26. John Paul II does not mean by this, however, that people do not bear God's image when they are alone, or that unmarried people somehow have a lessened version of God's image. He means, rather, that we can understand and express our human nature (our ability to know and love) most clearly in the outward expression of love, because we were made for communion with God and each other. This outward expression of charity does have a special quality within a marriage, a certain beauty that allows us to imagine what the inner harmony of the life of the Trinity might be like. And, when we learn to sacrifice

---

4   See *Summa Theologiae* I, q. 93, a. 9.

5   John Paul II, *Man and Woman He Created Them: A Theology of the Body,* trans. Michael Waldstein (Boston: Pauline Books & Media, 2006), 9:3. References are to the audience number and paragraph number.

and give ourselves to another within a marriage (of which we are capable due to our intellectual natures), we can learn also to practice Trinitarian love. For this reason, the Bible often uses the imagery of marriage to describe God's relationship to the people of Israel and to the Church. Perhaps the greatest example of this analogy is the Song of Songs, which is a love poem understood to be written about God's espousal to his people: "My beloved is mine, and I am his; he grazes among the lilies. Until the day breathes and the shadows flee, turn, my beloved, be like a gazelle or a young stag on cleft mountains" (Sg 2:17). The imagery of God as a young lover bounding over the mountains is surely striking and resonates with our experience of love in this life, allowing us a foretaste of the eternal love that awaits us in heaven. Marriage, therefore, is meant to serve as a lived sign of the marriage of Christ to his Church (and so of humanity to God, that is, of humanity to the Trinity). St. Paul writes of marriage: "'Therefore a man shall leave his father and mother and hold fast to his wife, and the two shall become one flesh.' This mystery is profound, and I am saying that it refers to Christ and the church" (Eph 5:31–32). Marriage is a sacrament, which means it is a sign that effects the grace that it signifies—it is a visible and concrete enactment of Christ's love for his Church. We can be trained in that love within the school of marriage, or we can learn from the witness of marriage even if we are not married ourselves.

However, outward expressions of charity are by no means limited to human marriage. Unmarried priests, nuns, and monks also live out this sign in a different mode. They dedicate their lives to the cultivation of charity in a way that is a powerful sign, a lived anticipation and embodiment of the espousal of humankind to God, because they are committed to marrying no one else. Their detachment from worldly possessions and ambitions is a sorely needed witness to an intellect that strives to dedicate its whole self to God in whose image it is made.

Especially in our modern world, where we are so enmeshed in the everyday demands of our work, our families, and the accumulation of wealth, it is easy to forget the perfection to which marriage is supposed to point, and vocations to the religious life serve as that unparalleled human witness. Perhaps we could say, following our distinction above, that marriage allows us to grasp the concreteness of being made in God's image, because it is such a tangible and fruitful communion of persons, but religious vocations help us to grasp what the perfection of that image—the likeness—could possibly be.

But we must remember that our ability to see the image of God in the living out of human life depends on seeing human nature as intellectual and as Godlike. Human expressions of charity are certainly not limited to either the vocation of marriage or religious vocations. By our baptism, we are called into the life of the Trinity and to bear witness to love of the Trinity in whatever form our lives end up taking, even if, for most, our baptismal vocation is perfected in a vow (i.e., in a wholehearted giving of ourselves). But if we fail to recognize the image of God in every person, we will fail to love every person as he ought to be loved—no matter what his state in life. Moreover, we can learn about Trinitarian love as it is expressed in all human interactions, and different human interactions can help us to see different dimensions of this love. One is not required to be married or a vowed religious to image God, and the freedom and potential of a single (i.e., unattached) person to love in diverse ways has its own particular character. As John Paul II writes, "Every individual is made in the image of God, insofar as he or she is a relational and free creature capable of knowing God and loving him . . . [but] being a person in the image and likeness of God thus also involves existing in a relationship, in a relation to the other 'I.'"[6] In other words, when we exist in

---

6   John Paul II, *Mulieris Dignitatem* (August 15, 1988), 7.

relationship, we show forth the image of God more radiantly, we work toward its perfection, but our dignity as human beings does not depend on our entering a vowed state.

Let's consider the image of God in a slightly different way. The above discussion could be summarized as follows: the primary way in which we image God is in the powers of our soul—our intellect and will—and the secondary way (or the further way, the particularly human way) in which we image God is by our bodies. To demonstrate the point, we can consider the fact that angels also image God because they have an intellectual nature (indeed, one superior to our own!), but they do not have bodies. They therefore image God in their own special way by their own particular mode of existence. It is likewise with human beings, because human beings also have a particular mode of existence, namely an existence that is a union of soul and body. We image God primarily in the powers of our soul (i.e., the intellect and will), but by body-soul unity we can say that the whole human person does image God. Imaging God by our whole person must, of course, presuppose the image found in the intellect, and this way of speaking does not imply that we look like God in a physical way, since God himself does not have a body for us to imitate. Once we acknowledge our intellectual nature, however, and what we were created for, then we can see how our bodily existence can be said to image God. For example, we can glimpse how begetting children is a vestige of the Trinity (as Son is begotten of the Father), or how our body-soul unity can image the presence of God everywhere in the world, because our soul is present in our whole body.[7] If we do not think about the image in this ordered way, however, we can quickly fall into the trap of making God in the image of man, rather than vice versa, and we can confuse our priorities in

---

7   See *Summa Theologiae* I, q. 93, a. 3.

striving to image God more fully. If, for example, we make the begetting of children our principal analogy for understanding the image of God—because the Father begets the Son and the Holy Spirit proceeds from them—then we would have to conclude that all animals capable of biological reproduction are also in God's image.

It is central to our faith that the image of God is given to every human being, even while we acknowledge that imaging God by our bodies or by our various postbaptismal vocations may help us toward perfecting that image. This point bears repeating because it is the foundation upon which a recognition of the dignity of human life is built. We can see this point clearly in Genesis 9, when God tells Noah that murder is prohibited because human beings are made in God's image:

> Whoever sheds the blood of man,
>   by man shall his blood be shed,
> for God made man in his own image. (Gn 9:6)

The principle laid out in this passage is that we must not destroy the life of an innocent person because that person is made in God's own image. Human life is sacred, therefore, not simply by divine decree, but because God has actually given his image to every human being. It is an act of sacrilege to attack another human being, because it is an attack on one who is like God. And, because we bear the image of God in our nature (not by how smart we are or by the vocation we choose), this image is possessed by all people. It is possessed, for example, by both young and old. The image does not develop over time nor fade away with time. The Church maintains the sanctity of all lives, of the unborn, of the sick, and of the elderly because, following Genesis 9, she recognizes in each person the image of God. The sanctity of the life of the disabled is also founded upon this theological principle.

Children do not have a vocation apart from the baptismal, and some disabled people are also not capable of sustaining a married life or a religious vocation, but children and the disabled image God and can receive baptism. In a culture that is becoming ever more utilitarian and efficient, we would do well to remember this lavish and unmerited gift of God given to all equally and thus to respect the life of every person we meet. If we fall prey to the idea that the image of God is found primarily by being in a marriage (for example), we may also begin to judge the worth of other people by some standard other than the one laid down by God himself. God has said that each human being has a life worthy of a share in his own. The inverse of this command in Genesis regarding murder is one stated many times by Jesus in the Gospels:

> You shall love the Lord your God with all your heart and with all your soul and with all your mind. This is the great and first commandment. And a second is like it: You shall love your neighbor as yourself. On these two commandments depend all the Law and the Prophets. (Mt 22:38–40)

When we love God fully, we also love his image in our neighbor. These two commandments are joined at the hip. To think that we can love God without love of neighbor is to think we can somehow love God without loving the reflection of him in our midst. And, like in the Genesis passage, where blood is shed at a one-to-one ratio, so is love given and received in an equal trade; we owe to others as much love and respect as we owe to ourselves, because all are made in God's image.

That human beings are made in the image of God, therefore, takes on fullness of meaning when we know both who God is and the love of the Trinity to which we are aspiring to unite ourselves. And it was in order to renew the image of God in us that Jesus Christ came in the flesh. Let us keep in mind therefore the nature God gave us and the life he intended for us as we turn to the doctrine of the Incarnation.

11

The Bible and the Incarnation

From the doctrine of the Trinity and the meaning of humankind, we naturally move to the doctrine of the Incarnation. Even if you are not familiar with the word "incarnation," you are already familiar with the concept, because we could not have gotten this far without having mentioned it. The Incarnation (literally "enfleshment") refers to the mystery of the second person of the Trinity (the Son, the Word) becoming a human being in the person of Jesus Christ. The term "incarnation" comes from a passage that we have already discussed in brief: "And the Word became flesh and dwelt among us" (Jn 1:14). As we saw earlier, the conflict with Arius in the fourth century was a controversy about whether or not Jesus was fully divine, and the creed of Nicea, written in the midst of this controversy, paved the way for a full expression of the doctrine of the Trinity. However, once it was proclaimed that Christ could and should be called consubstantial with the Father, another important question logically followed (and historically, another controversy as well). If Christ is God—as God the Father is God—transcendent, infinite, and unchangeable, how could he possibly become flesh? Doesn't this imply a change of the divine nature? Is it possible for Christ to be fully human if he is God? In this chapter, we will turn to the biblical text and see that there are just as many passages that portray Jesus as wholly human, and acting as one of us, as there are passages where Jesus is divine and acting like God. In fact, there are many passages where Jesus's apparently divine actions appear alongside his apparently human ones. This tension will present us with another theological mystery to ponder: how is it possible for God to become man, and why would he do so?

There are many challenging passages that reveal Jesus as truly human, sometimes in ways that seem incompatible with his divinity. For example, Jesus experiences all forms of human emotion. When his friend Lazarus died, we are told that Jesus responded as any human being would:

> Now when Mary came to where Jesus was and saw him, she fell at his feet, saying to him, "Lord, if you had been here, my brother would not have died." When Jesus saw her weeping, and the Jews who had come with her also weeping, he was deeply moved in his spirit and greatly troubled. And he said, "Where have you laid him?" They said to him, "Lord, come and see." Jesus wept. (Jn 11:32–35)

This passage is moving, but it does not seem to correspond to what we know of God. Jesus not only weeps for the death of his friend, but he seems to be moved to pity and weeping by the sight of Lazarus's mourning sister. God, as we know, is unchangeable. He cannot be unexpectedly moved to pity (properly speaking) by the sorrow of another. Here Jesus exhibits that most human of emotions: grief. How can he who gives life have grief at the sight of death? And, if he knows all things, how could Jesus seem to be suddenly overcome by emotion? Some of the onlookers in the story have these same kinds of questions, and doubt Jesus's power. If he is the Christ, they ask, if he has the power to heal the blind, couldn't he have stopped Lazarus from dying (cf. Jn 11:37)?

And yet, in this same story, we also witness one of Jesus's most powerful miracles and have an affirmation of his wholly divine character. Jesus knows already that Lazarus has died before he comes to the house and has already announced that he would raise him, saying, "Our friend Lazarus has fallen asleep, but I go to awaken him" (Jn 11:11). The disciples, by the way, need to have it explained to them explicitly that Jesus means that Lazarus has died (Jn 11:12–14). Jesus even says that he is glad for Lazarus's death so that this death might be an occasion to perform a miracle and therefore for others to come to faith. He sees the role that the death of Lazarus will play in the plan of salvation. Moreover, when Jesus arrives in Bethany and speaks to Martha, Lazarus's sister, he again proclaims himself to be equal to the creator.

> Martha said to Jesus, "Lord, if you had been here, my brother would not have died. But even now I know that whatever you ask from God, God will give you." Jesus said to her, "Your brother will rise again." Martha said to him, "I know that he will rise again in the resurrection on the last day." Jesus said to her, "I am the resurrection and the life. Whoever believes in me, though he die, yet shall he live, and everyone who lives and believes in me shall never die. Do you believe this?" She said to him, "Yes, Lord; I believe that you are the Christ, the Son of God, who is coming into the world." (Jn 11:21–27)

When Martha professes faith in Christ's ability to gain whatever he asks from God, Jesus challenges her even further. He asks her not whether she believes in the resurrection of the dead only, but whether she believes that he, Jesus, *is* the resurrection and the life. By calling himself the life, Jesus once again evokes Exodus 3 and the name of God as "I AM." He is asking Martha whether she believes not only that Christ has the power to raise the dead because he is close to God, but whether she believes that he *is* God, that he is Life itself. That is why Martha's response is no longer a profession of faith in

Jesus's power or the fact of the Resurrection, but a confession of faith in Jesus's person, as the Christ, the Son of God ("Yes, Lord; I believe you are the Christ"). Here, our questions come to a head: How can the one who weeps be the Life? Is Jesus's weeping only an act for our benefit, or was he truly sad?

Another story that poses the same kinds of questions is the raising of the son of the widow of Nain (Lk 7:11–17). In this story, Jesus and his disciples are approaching the town of Nain when they see a funeral procession. The man who has died is the only son of a widow. Luke tells us that "when the Lord saw her, he had compassion on her and said to her, 'Do not weep.' Then he came up and touched the bier, and the bearers stood still. And he said, 'Young man, I say to you, arise'" (Lk 7:13–14). Here again, Jesus seems to be emotionally moved and affected by the pain of others. In this story, Jesus's humanity is perhaps even more apparent, as surely he is moved by the mourning of a widow who has to look upon the body of her only son because he sees the fate of his own mother. But again, as in the story of the raising of Lazarus, he exhibits the power of God by reviving the man at a touch.

There are many other stories where Jesus shows human emotion and weakness. Jesus hungers (e.g., Mt 4:1) and thirsts (e.g., Jn 19:28), and he eats and drinks even after his Resurrection (Jn 21:12–13). He gets tired (e.g., Jn 4:6). There is one scene in particular where it is hard to think that Jesus experiences sadness in appearance only, which is in the account of the agony in the garden of Gethsemane, as Christ prepares for the suffering of the cross:

> And they went to a place called Gethsemane. And he said to his disciples, "Sit here while I pray." And he took with him Peter and James and John, and began to be greatly distressed and troubled. And he said to them, "My soul is very sorrowful, even to death. Remain here and watch." And going a little farther, he fell on the

ground and prayed that, if it were possible, the hour might pass from him. And he said, "Abba, Father, all things are possible for you. Remove this cup from me. Yet not what I will, but what you will." (Mk 14:32–36)

Here, Jesus seems to be at the end of his rope. His disciples are falling asleep rather than comforting him. He says he is experiencing such sadness that it is likened to death. He begs God the Father that he should not have to die, as we beg God in prayer when we are in distress. How can God himself be in such a state, and is Christ's will not the same as the Father's will?

In addition to the human emotion that Jesus displays, we also see him facing the same kinds of challenges that other human beings face. We are told, for example, that immediately following his baptism, Jesus was tempted in the wilderness by the devil. Is there a point in tempting God? Nevertheless, the temptations seem real enough. Jesus is hungry and tempted to eat. Jesus, who is headed to death on a cross, is tempted with power over his own life. Jesus, who is going to have a rather unreliable band of twelve disciples, is tempted with all the kingdoms of the world (see the account of the temptations in Mt 4:1–11). As the letter to the Hebrews says, "[W]e do not have a high priest who is unable to sympathize with our weaknesses, but one who in every respect has been tempted as we are, yet without sin" (Heb 4:15). It seems strange that the God of the universe could be tempted as a human being by food and power, but Hebrews seems to insist that Jesus is like us because he has undergone human temptation.

Perhaps some of the most challenging passages are ones where Jesus speaks of his own relationship to the Father as one that appears to be unequal. In Matthew's Gospel, after predicting the signs of the end of the age and the future passing away of heaven and earth, Jesus says, "But concerning that day and hour no one knows, not even the angels of heaven, nor the Son, but the Father only" (Mt 24:36). Here it appears that although Jesus is putting himself a little above the angels he is below the Father. If Christ is God, is he not omniscient, and aware of all things in the mind of the Father? Likewise, in the verse just before John 10:30, where Jesus says explicitly than he and the Father are one, Jesus also says that the Father is greater than all, from which he does not seem to exclude himself (Jn 10:29). Later in that same Gospel, Christ says he is departing and going to the Father because "the Father is greater than I" (Jn 14:28). If we have seen in the previous few chapters why Christ is called consubstantial with the Father from both scriptural and traditional sources, we must now come to see how the Father can possibly be called greater than the Son.

What precipitated the controversy about the relationship between Jesus's humanity and his divinity (often called the "Christological controversy"), however, was not any of these verses in particular. Rather, it was the simple fact of Jesus having a mother. By the fifth century, the title for Mary "Mother of God" (or *theotokos* in Greek) had long been in use in the Christian East and was especially beloved among Egyptian Christians. However, a popular preacher named Nestorius, who was the bishop of Constantinople (arguably the most important city in the Roman empire at that time), publicly denounced the use of this name as superstitious. "[A] Greek without reproach introducing mothers for the gods!"[1] he preached in 428. Nestorius reasoned that God, being immortal and uncaused, did not have a mother. Calling Mary the "Mother of God" sounded to his ears like a Greek myth, like saying Zeus is the father of the demi-God Hercules or Hera is the mother of Ares. Nestorius proposed instead we should

---

1   Nestorius, "First Sermon of Nestorius against the Theotokos," in *The Christological Controversy*, trans. Richard A. Norris (Minneapolis: Fortress Press, 1980), 124.

call Mary *Christotokos*, the mother of Christ, because the divine nature has no mother and has always been in existence. His debate with Cyril of Alexandria, who defended the use of this title, resulted in a major theological disagreement and prompted the writing of the Chalcedonian definition (to be discussed in the next chapter), which spells out the relationship between Jesus's humanity and his divinity.

But the origins of this debate should perhaps serve to remind us that the heart of the mystery (and the scandal) of the Incarnation is in the mere fact of God being born, of God coming among us. Jesus shows emotion, is tempted, experiences human limitation, and indeed he suffers and dies. St. Ignatius of Antioch, a martyr of the second century, puts this mystery to us boldly by calling the blood of Christ simply "the blood of God."[2] Does God, the immortal, have blood? But to start even before the cross, how can God be born? How can God have a mother as we do, and why in the world would he want to be born as we are to live the kind of lives we lead? How, finally, do we understand "the Word became flesh and dwelt among us" (Jn 1:14)? Augustine meditates on the mystery of Jesus's nativity by reflecting on the humility of the Word becoming one who cannot speak. He plays on the Latin word "*infans,*" which means a baby, but it also means one who is incapable of speech. He begins one of his Christmas homilies by saying, "It is called the Lord's birthday when the Wisdom of God presented itself to us as an infant (*infantem*), and the Word of God without words uttered the flesh as its voice."[3] To be a baby and to have a mother, to have a birthday, seems wholly unfitting to God. To be small, weak, completely defenseless seems the antithesis of God's very being. To be forced to flee from one's enemies, as Jesus

---

2   Ignatius of Antioch, *Letter to the Ephesians,* in *The Apostolic Fathers,* trans. Michael Holmes (Grand Rapids, Mich.: Baker, 2007), 1.1.

3   Augustine, *Sermons,* trans. Edmund Hill, vol. 6 (Brooklyn: New City Press, 1993), 185.1.

fled to Egypt to escape the plans of Herod (cf. Mt 2:13–14), does not become the almighty God! Yet, the Bible presents us with a God who, in Christ, does become a baby, unable to speak, who nurses from his mother and experiences human life as every one of us does, except without sin. In response to Nestorius's challenge, the Church must therefore develop a language to speak about Christ in a way that affirms that he is the one who is consubstantial with the Father, and yet he is the one who on earth has a mother. To these formulations we now turn.

1 2

Christ Is Fully God and Fully Man

The preaching of Nestorius against the use of the word "*theotokos*" did not end with one single homily, but was a prolonged back-and-forth between Nestorius (in Constantinople) and Cyril of Alexandria (in Egypt). The exchange went on for many years until a theological solution was reached at the Council of Chalcedon in 451.[1] The council produced a statement that incorporated both the insights of those sympathetic to Nestorius, as well as the Egyptians who opposed him. But what were those insights?

Nestorius, as we have already seen, was concerned with the transcendence of God. He did not see how God could be said to become fully human without in some way compromising the immutability of God, and without damaging our notion of God as completely other than the created world. Nestorius did not deny that Christ was God, but he wanted to keep Christ's humanity at a distance from the divine nature. He therefore liked to speak of Christ as being in some way "dual." For Nestorius, Christ has two natures, human and divine, but these two could not possibly be mixed up with one another, since the divine nature is immutable and always whole. As

---

1   Although the formula was a combination of Alexandrian and Antiochene ideas, accepted in East and West, some Egyptians still rejected the formula as being too Nestorian. The council of Chalcedon therefore resulted in the first major Christian schism, from which arose the (now called) Coptic church in Egypt. Part of the reason for this falling out is that Cyril himself died before the meeting of the council.

we saw in the last chapter, Christ behaves both as God and man, but he cannot be half and half or a mixture, since the divine nature is unmixable. The problem with Nestorius's way of thinking was that he seemed to lack a good way of speaking about how Christ was still *one* despite having two natures. Therefore, Nestorius was accused of introducing the idea that there were actually two different sons, the son of God and the son of Mary. It was for this reason that Nestorius wished to speak of the human Jesus (but not the divine Son) being born of Mary, thereby denying Mary the title "Mother of God." The proper insight of Nestorius, and those who thought like him, therefore, was that Christ must in some way be *two*, but he failed to spell out how Christ was still only *one*. The idea that there could be a son of Mary other than the one Christ who is God is just too abstract; it does not correspond to the reality that there is only one Jesus Christ.

Cyril, along with other Egyptians, insisted on the unity of Christ's person. They were suspicious of Nestorius speaking so much of two, since it seemed to deny that there was only one Christ and that he was God. Any attempt to divide Christ made the Egyptians worried that Christ would become incoherent, not fully one person, or that the Christ who lived and walked on the earth was somehow not truly God in the flesh. They feared, in other words, that Christ would be seen as a human being who was somehow adopted by God or just a person helped out by the Word, rather than as God-become-man as John 1:14 teaches. Cyril wanted to make sure that Christ was seen as one person, the one person who speaks and acts in the Gospels, one Lord. After all, if we worship Christ, he must be God, not a man whom God endorses or even a man with whom God unites himself, since worship is due to God alone. The insight of Cyril, then, is that there is only *one* Christ and he must be God.

What resulted at the council of Chalcedon was that Christ was declared to have a twoness as well as a oneness.

In short, the formula for speaking about Christ's humanity and divinity is that Christ is *one* person with *two* natures. Our previous discussions of the words "person" and "nature" in the context of the doctrine of the Trinity should be of some help here. Christ has two natures, two *whats*. A nature dictates what someone can do, and so Christ can and does act according to two different *whats*. Speaking of Christ having two natures helps to explain all those biblical passages where Jesus acts as a human being and also as a divine person within the same story. He can and does act according to both of his natures. But, Christ is only one person, only one *who*. Against Nestorius, the council of Chalcedon proclaimed that there is only one subject and that Christ as a human being cannot be spoken of as a separate person from the divine Christ. Let's look at the formula of Chalcedon section by section to see how this compromise was reached and how the mystery of the Incarnation is expressed by the Church:

> Therefore, following the holy fathers, we confess one and the same Son, who is our Lord Jesus Christ, and we all agree in teaching that this very same Son is complete in his deity and complete—the very same—in his humanity, truly God and truly a human being . . .[2]

Here, the opening line of the definition affirms the desire of the council to follow but clarify what was laid down at Nicea (i.e., the teaching that Christ is consubstantial with the Father). In order to do this, as well as to give us the complete picture of the Christ of the Gospels, the council declares Christ to be *fully God and fully man* (using the words "complete" and "truly"). Nestorius's insight that the divine nature cannot exist mashed

---

2   This translation of the definition of Chalcedon is taken from *The Christological Controversy*, trans. Richard A. Norris (Minneapolis: Fortress Press, 1980), 159.

up or in parts is taken into account, because Christ possesses two entire and complete natures. The council continues:

> this very same one being composed of a rational soul and body; coessential with the Father as to his deity, and coessential with us—the very same one—as to his humanity; being like us in all respects, apart from sin . . .

The definition continues to specify that Christ is a human being, and not in appearance only. He is not merely God who wears his manhood like a spacesuit, nor is he the apparition of a man, but he is a whole and entire human being with soul and body. He is wholly human and shares his human nature with us; he is wholly God and shares his divine nature (or substance) with the Father. The definition goes on:

> as to his deity, he was born from the Father before the ages, but as to his humanity—the very same one was born in the last days from the Virgin Mary, the Mother of God (*theotokos*), for our sake and for our salvation . . .

Again clarifying the distinction of the two natures, the definition explains that the divine nature was not given its birth by Mary. The Word was begotten outside of time, before all ages. And yet, Mary can be called the "Mother of God"(the *theotokos*) because she did give birth to the God-man in the flesh. The reason for this was not because God needed human birth, but was "for our sake and for our salvation." Put otherwise: Mary gave birth to Christ and he is God. Therefore, she can be called "Mother of God," even while we acknowledge that the divine nature is without beginning. And so the one born of the *theotokos* is:

> one and the same Christ, Son, Lord, Only-begotten, acknowledged to be unconfusedly, unalterably, undividedly,

> inseparably in two natures; since the difference of the natures is not destroyed because of the union, but on the contrary, the character of each nature is preserved and comes together in one person and one hypostasis, not divided or torn into two persons but one and the same Son and only-begotten God, Logos, Lord Jesus Christ . . .

This section can be a bit overwhelming at first! But it is here that the insights of both Nestorius and Cyril are wonderfully harmonized. Christ is described as *two* so that the divine nature remains unchanged and can be held as distinct from the human nature, but Christ is said to be only *one* person ("hypostasis" being a Greek word for "person," left untranslated in the text). The unity of Christ is made clear, especially by the repetition of the phrase "the very same one" throughout the definition. You can see the back and forth between expressions of twoness and oneness at every turn. Christ has two natures. These two are not confused with one another nor are they changed ("unconfusedly, unalterably") because the divine and human natures cannot be mixed or mutated. And yet, the two natures are also not separated ("undividedly, inseparably") because Christ is one person. The two natures can be distinguished and each nature remains whole ("character of each nature is preserved"). And yet, the two come together in such perfect unity that there is only "one and the same Son"—only one person.

There are two technical theological terms that help to capture everything that the definition of Chalcedon teaches. The first one is "hypostatic union," which is a fancy way of saying "union of person," since the word "hypostasis," as said above, means "person." This phrase is shorthand for saying that the two natures are so united in Christ that he is only one. The mechanism for how this works (i.e., how this perfect unity is possible) is ultimately a mystery. The definition of Chalcedon and the rather scientific sounding phrase "hypostatic union" only aim to represent the mystery in as precise language as possible, in part so that we can name it and discuss it. How can it be that two natures so different can coexist perfectly in one single person without being mixed but also without separation? In an "unspeakable and unutterable" way, answers Cyril of Alexandria.[3] In other words, we do not know or presume to be able to explain the *how* of Christ's inner life, but we do profess the mystery of his life, based on who he is and what he teaches about himself in the Gospel. The hypostatic union is the union of two natures in one person.

The other term that is useful to add to our theological encyclopedia is "the communication of idioms," which is taken directly from Latin and means "sharing of properties." This phrase summarizes the truth that, because of the unity accomplished by the hypostatic union (the two natures unified in the one person of Christ), anything that is said of Christ as human can be said also of Christ as divine. Christ is, after all, only one person, agent, and subject. When you say anything about Christ, you are only talking about one person, not two different people. It is finally because of this theological principle that we can say that Mary is "Mother of God." Not because Mary gives birth to God in the primeval past (like Hera or Aphrodite), but because she gives birth to the one who is God, and what is said of his humanity (his birth in time) can be said also of the same subject who is divine. The upshot of the entire controversy is that Mary retains her title as the *theotokos*. God is born on Christmas day!

Having now grappled with the hypostatic union and the communication of idioms, we know the proper Christological language of the Church. The Christ of the Gospels who is moved with compassion but also raises the dead is one who is fully God and fully man. He possesses two natures completely

---

3   Cyril of Alexandria, "Second Letter to Nestorius," in ibid., 133.

and entirely in his one person, and he acts according to those natures. He is not human in appearance only, but is human like us, with body and soul. Conversely, Christ is not just adopted by God nor is he simply a really holy person, but he is God, consubstantial with the Father. In short, the mystery of the Incarnation is that God became man, or, as Chalcedon makes crystal clear, one who is truly God became truly man. By the hypostatic union, the two natures of Christ are united. And by the communication of idioms, what is said of Christ can be said of God, because Christ is God.

As with the doctrine of the Trinity, we should speak of this mystery as best we can with the words of the tradition, so carefully laid out, to maintain the mystery of Christ's person. But, by using analogies, we can also attempt to attain a deeper level of understanding of it by comparison with familiar things. The primary analogy that the Church Fathers use to explain the unity of the human and divine in Christ is that of a soul's unity with the body. It may at first seem like two natures cannot quite "fit" in one person, since all the people we know only have one nature, but the Fathers point out that it also might not seem like a soul could "fit" in a body. Where is there room for the soul in our bodies? But thinking in this way would cause us to miss the kind of unity a soul has with the body, which is not spatial or physical. The soul somehow permeates the entire body—there is just as much soul in your big toe as in your brain—and yet, the soul is not blended or mixed up with the body. It animates the body but can be distinguished from the body. Although in the modern world we do not tend to speak about the soul as much, the analogy can help us imagine a unity that could occur without confusion and without change, but also without separation.

Another way the Church Fathers sometimes speak of Christ's body is as an instrument. They do not mean by this that Christ's body is just an external tool he uses to get things done, because Christ's body is his own (just as our bodies are our own). Rather, they are trying to communicate that Christ inhabits and uses the body to carry out the will of God. If we think about what it is like to play a musical instrument with a high level of proficiency (or if you have ever seen a concert violinist play, for example), you can imagine the kind of unity the musician has with this instrument, and how the music flows from his inner being to be outwardly expressed by the instrument. Now, in the case of Christ, imagine one person who is able to play two instruments at once (perhaps like the case of a folk musician who plays harmonica and guitar simultaneously). These two instruments, although distinct and discrete, can be used to play the same song, and they can be in perfect harmony, just as Christ acted with two natures with complete consistency. Christ is not incoherent, but has one unified expression of his two natures. This analogy is different from the view of Nestorius, which would be more like two people sitting side-by-side playing a duet on the piano. The analogy falls short in many ways, since the instruments in this case are different from the musician; whereas Christ *is* one person with two natures, he does not just hold or wield two natures. The two instruments can also be divided, unlike Christ's natures. Nevertheless, perhaps in the image of one musician playing two instruments perfectly and in tandem, we can see how it is possible for there to exist a person who is capable of possessing and expressing the characteristics of two natures at the same time.

The imagery of music and harmony leads us to reflect on the fact that the doctrine of the Incarnation is not only a great mystery, but sublime and beautiful. It is one of the chief subjects of Christian wonder and awe. This mystery is therefore frequently meditated upon in the Church's music and in her poetry. Indeed, as mentioned earlier, the famous passage about the Incarnation found in Philippians 2:5–11 (Christ "emptied himself, by taking the form of a servant") is thought to be taken from an early Christian hymn. A part of this Pauline hymn is often sung on Palm Sunday (its Latin title is *Christus factus est*). Consider also the first stanza of the Eucharistic hymn "Let All Mortal Flesh Keep Silence," a nineteenth-century hymn (based on the fourth-century liturgy of St. James):

> Let all mortal flesh keep silence,
> And with fear and trembling stand;
> Ponder nothing earthly-minded,
> For with blessing in His hand,
> Christ our God to earth descendeth,
> Our full homage to demand.

The hymn captures the reverence with which we should regard the Incarnation. That it was our mortal flesh assumed by Christ should cause us to turn in worship to God (in homage, as the hymn says), but also to be struck silent knowing that it is our own humanity that the Lord came to save. Not in appearance only did God come among us. The hymn goes on to remind us that the Incarnation is the cause of our being able to participate in the Eucharist:

> King of kings, yet born of Mary,
> As of old on earth He stood,
> Lord of lords, in human vesture,
> In the body and the blood;
> He will give to all the faithful
> His own self for heav'nly food.

Echoing the council of Chalcedon, the hymn declares that Christ is almighty king of the universe, and yet endured a human birth from Mary. It is because he truly took on body and blood that we can therefore eat his Body and Blood as heavenly food in the Mass. The Eucharist as we understand it cannot exist without the Incarnation.

We can think also of many Christmas carols that implore us to worship a mere baby, because we recognize in that baby not just some person without sin, or even a great prophet, but God himself, born as a common human being. You will hear many echoes of the creed and even the Chalcedonian definition in these hymns that attempt to express the wonder of Christmas. The Christmas story is not just a heartwarming tale involving a star, some kings, and a few donkeys. It is for this reason that our mortal flesh trembles and remains silent. It is for this reason that we should "fall on our knees" (as "O, Holy Night" would have it) and that we should "hail the incarnate deity" (as "Hark the Herald Angels Sing" implores).

By expressions of praise, these hymns try to do justice to the mystery that was defined by the council of Chalcedon. Without this crucial clarification, we would not fully understand who lay in the manger. We would not understand the Jesus of the Gospels. But there still remain many questions pertaining to the Incarnation and its purpose. Why, after all, did God become a human being in the first place? And beyond articulating clearly how Jesus can behave the way he does in the Gospels, what difference does it really make whether Jesus is the God-man or whether he is some kind of perfect creation? Could God not have saved us by a prophet or sinless person? Could God not have saved us without the indignity of becoming a human being? Our hymns have already hinted at some of the answers to these questions, and the cause of the Incarnation will be the subject of the next two chapters.

13

Why God Was Born

In the previous two chapters, we have been discussing how Christ acts in the New Testament, and the conclusion to which early Christians came about this Christ: that he is fully God and fully man. But what was the cause of God coming among us as a human being in the way that he did? In the opening of the third part of the *Summa*, Thomas Aquinas lists around ten distinct reasons for the Incarnation, adding at the end of his list that "there are very many other advantages which accrued, above man's apprehension."[1] In other words, the Incarnation is the perfect solution to the human problem (and even more).

The origin of the human problem—the fact that we, despite being made in the image of God, are selfish and sinful—is described in Genesis 3. In this story, Adam and Eve disobey the one law laid down by God, the command not to eat of the tree of the knowledge of good and evil. The particular details of this story have been the subject of much theological reflection. For example, there have been many answers given to the question of what the tree is meant to represent, and why Adam and Eve would have committed such a sin, but the result of this act at the beginning of human history is clear: we lost our original relationship with God. By reaching for

---

1   *Summa Theologiae* III, q. 1, a. 2.

what was forbidden, by claiming that which was wrong for us to have, we lost what we should have been. The penalty in Genesis is also clear: "You shall not eat of the fruit of the tree that is in the midst of the garden, neither shall you touch it, lest you die" (Gn 3:3). By failing to be in harmony with Life itself (i.e., with God), we decided to become our own first principle. But, since we are only made in the image of God, we are not eternal ourselves. We are not the source of our own existence, and therefore we are now tending back toward the nothing from which God brought us. We are now corruptible, capable of wasting away. We are now mortal and we are selfish, rather than being immortal and self-giving. To recall a distinction made in an earlier chapter, we do still bear the image of God in our rational soul, but we do not bear the likeness of God. Put otherwise, this image of God in us is damaged and tarnished. Therefore, our ability to share in the life of the Trinity is likewise impaired, since to be made in the image means to be capable of knowing and loving God.

Athanasius, in his famous work *On the Incarnation*, casts this Fall of humankind in the terms of a dilemma for God. On the one hand, it would not make sense if creatures with whom God intended to share his life were simply to pass out of existence. In that case, it would have been better for us never to have been created at all. Could our creation really be called good (as it is in Genesis), after all, if we were to sin and then be annihilated? On the other hand, it would be a violation of our freedom and of God's justice to erase our sin and its effects. God had said that the penalty of sin was death, and God does not lie. That sin causes death, however, is not merely the result of God's word, an arbitrary law that God must uphold just because he said so. Rather, sin does in fact result in death because sin is separation from God (who is the ground of existence) by a free act. In short, when we reject the Life, we die. Even if Adam and Eve had repented immediately, the damage that their sin had caused would remain, because they truly were created free and their acts have true consequences. And, although it is of course not outside God's power to restore us instantly by a divine command, to do so would circumvent our free will—the same free will that makes us like God in the first place. God's plan for the world, therefore, appears thwarted, since he desires to have the love of free human beings, and it seems that either our existence or our freedom would have to be sacrificed to resolve the problem of sin.

The solution to this divine dilemma—if you had not already begun to guess—is the Incarnation. One who is fully God and fully man is able to resolve this seeming conflict between love and justice, and to heal the human condition. In order to understand why the Incarnation is the appropriate answer to the problem of sin, Athanasius separates the effects of the Incarnation into two categories, which we will discuss in this chapter and the next: Christ restores the image of God in us (discussed in this chapter), and Christ overcomes sin and death (discussed in the next).

Christ by his Incarnation restores the image of God in us. If Adam and Eve severed their relationship with God and tarnished our spiritual likeness to him, how can we regain it? Restoration of the image is not something that we could work hard to get for ourselves, nor could we obtain it from some other creature, since the image belongs to God himself and to no one else. Such an attempt would be like trying to make a copy of a painting that has been lost; you would never be able to get it quite right, even if you knew the subject of the painting to some degree. Nor could God simply restore the image by snapping his fingers without in some sense disregarding the free choice of Adam and Eve to turn away. Such a renewal could hardly be said to be one that came from within the human race, and would at best be an external imposition by God. But God's power, as we know, is not the kind of power that competes with human agency, and it is not merely a heightened version of human power (i.e., not like the kind of power that we use to get what we want by force). And, since God is all-knowing and all-powerful, his original plan for humankind cannot be defeated by human actions. Therefore, God also desires to renew the image already given to us, not to make a whole new image or to start over with some fresh creature, as if our creation had just been one big mistake. Who, therefore, was capable of renewing the image? God alone. But in whom did the image need to be remade? Humankind. Therefore, one who is fully God and fully man came to restore the truly divine image in a truly human person. This restoration was fittingly undertaken by the Word of God, the second person of the Trinity, because, if we recall what we learned about the doctrine of the Trinity, the Son is spoken of as God's perfect self-representation, his thought, "the image of the invisible God" (Col 1:15). Our image is restored by the one who is God's absolute image, "the exact imprint of his nature" (Heb 1:3).

There are two ways in which we can understand how Christ's birth restores the image in us: internally and externally. Internally, our image is renewed simply by virtue of God becoming man. By taking on flesh, Christ who is the perfect image of God, redraws the original image on a human canvas. Christ brings that lost painting back into the world so that we may become a copy of it once again. Athanasius uses a similar analogy. If a canvas on which a portrait is painted becomes tarnished, how can the painting be restored? The only way to ensure it is painted properly is if the original subject of the portrait comes into the studio to sit again for the artist. Likewise, to renew the image of God in humankind, the original subject of that image had to appear. Except that in the case of Christ the restoration is even more complete, because the one who is the image is also the artist; he is the creator who made both the portrait and the medium upon which it was drawn. Christ therefore restores human nature and gives us back the possibility of perfection by taking our nature to himself. As Paul tells us, "Therefore, if anyone is in Christ, he is a new creation. The old has passed away; behold, the new has come" (2 Cor 5:17). For this reason, Christmas day is such a high feast! Not only is Christ born into the world so that he can eventually die for us when he grows up, but his very birth gives us back something that was lost.

Externally, moreover, Christ renewed the image by living a perfect human life, and he became for us the model of holiness. We can read about his public life in the Gospels. We can know how he prayed and spoke. We can imitate what he did in our moral and spiritual lives. We therefore have an image that not only renews and cleanses us from within, but an image that is set before our eyes—a real human person, with flesh and blood. For this reason, we continue to depict Christ in art, and contemplate him with our eyes, because God chose to depict himself for the sake of those who learn by the senses and learn by experience. Athanasius describes Christ's human life—his miracles and actions performed in the body—as the perfect cure for idolatry. Idolatry is not only the chief sin of humankind throughout the Old Testament but also of Adam and Eve, because idolatry is putting something in the created world in place of God, or loving something created more than the creator. In our current sinful state, we are painfully addicted to created things (money, food, or, worst of all, ourselves). Christ came among created things so that our longing for the tangible world could be fulfilled by one who is also divine. Christ became the idol who is no idol at all, because he is God.

But perhaps one of the most striking mysteries about Jesus's real human life is his hidden life, that is, all the time

Jesus spent on earth about which the Gospels tell us precious little. In this mundane life, Jesus is an example to us in a powerful way. Jesus was thirty when he began his public ministry, and apart from the stories about his infancy and the finding of Jesus in the temple at age twelve (Lk 2:41–52), we know almost nothing about this early life. The *Catechism* says of this time that "during the greater part of his life Jesus shared the condition of the vast majority of human beings: a daily life spent without evident greatness, a life of manual labour. His religious life was that of a Jew obedient to the law of God, a life in the community."[2] Because Jesus lived this normal life, as a person like any other in his community, those in his hometown questioned him and his authority:

> They were astonished, and said, "Where did this man get this wisdom and these mighty works? Is not this the carpenter's son? Is not his mother called Mary? And are not his brothers James and Joseph and Simon and Judas? And are not all his sisters with us? Where then did this man get all these things?" And they took offense at him. (Mt 13:54–57)

The people in Nazareth took Jesus for granted because he truly entered into boring old human life. But we must not think of this hiddenness as just a blank, something unimportant that the Gospel writers left out because it is of little interest. Rather, in this quiet life of Jesus we can see that it was precisely ordinary human life that he came to sanctify. Jesus obeyed his parents (Lk 2:51). He grew up (Lk 2:52). We know therefore that the renewal of the image in us and the pursuit of holiness does not require that we live a life that is anything other than ordinary, but we must learn to live whatever life we are given as Christ would have lived it. Christ calls us all to greatness even in our

---

2   *CCC*, 531.

smallness. As Paul says, "[Y]ou know the grace of our Lord Jesus Christ, that though he was rich, yet for your sake he became poor, so that you by his poverty might become rich" (2 Cor 8:9).

Another way to think about this renewal of the image (both internal and external) is to think of Christ as the new Adam. Paul describes Christ as reversing the deed of Adam in a number of places, for example, in the letter to the Romans:

> Therefore, as one trespass led to condemnation for all men, so one act of righteousness leads to justification and life for all men. For as by the one man's disobedience the many were made sinners, so by the one man's obedience the many will be made righteous. (Rom 5:18–19)

Christ, by being born human, became the new head of the human race; he recapitulated humanity ("recapitulate" meaning to re-head, but also to summarize). Before Christ, the summary of human life was the one Adam gave us, the one of failure and pride. We were under the condemnation of his trespass, as Paul says. But, because Christ lived in every way as we do and yet was without sin (cf. Heb 4:15), he renewed and redefined what is possible for a human being to be. He lived as the true image and likeness of God. He succeeded where Adam failed, being obedient where Adam was disobedient. He died on the tree rather than steal from it. Christ, then, by recapitulating the human race, made it possible once again for us to be what we were supposed to be, and gave us a renewed humanity to which we could cling. That is why we are baptized: to have a second birth from the lineage of the new Adam, a supernatural birth that frees us from the condemnation inherited from the old Adam. We then become inheritors of the grace of Christ, the grace to grow into the perfect image that Christ is, the image that he also put on display for us in his life on earth.

By his renewal of the image, both by taking our nature and by teaching us, Christ restores to us knowledge of the Father. The renewal of the image is intimately related to the renewing of our minds, because to be in God's image means to be able to know him completely, as we discussed in chapter 9. So, Paul urges us: "Do not be conformed to this world, but be transformed by the renewal of your mind" (Rom 12:2). Christ therefore teaches us about the Father in his earthly teaching and in his miracles, while at the same time embodying this perfect knowledge by taking on our flesh. He is a human being who fully knows the Father and reveals the Father. This part of Christ's mission is made especially clear in the Gospel of John.

> Philip said to him, "Lord, show us the Father, and it is enough for us." Jesus said to him, "Have I been with you so long, and you still do not know me, Philip? Whoever has seen me has seen the Father. How can you say, 'Show us the Father'? Do you not believe that I am in the Father and the Father is in me? The words that I say to you I do not speak on my own authority, but the Father who dwells in me does his works." (Jn 14:8–10)

In this passage, Jesus so strongly identifies himself with the Father that he says we can see the Father by looking at him. Our knowledge can be renewed by gazing upon Christ, because Christ reveals God to us and renews our intellect from within that we may know God again. In his very person, Christ heals the breach between God and man because he is both. He makes possible an eternal relationship with God by showing us who God is, and by showing us who we can be.

The renewal of knowledge is therefore chiefly a renewal of the knowledge of the love of God—of God's love for us and of his love dwelling within us. This love is what Adam and Eve seem to have doubted in the garden, rejecting that God's command was out of love rather than some other motivation, and it is in love that Adam and Eve subsequently failed, since the punishment of their sin is removal from the garden and from the presence of God (cf. Gn 3:23), and broken relations with one another (cf. Gn 3:16). In Christ, it is not just facts about God's nature that become real to us by his revelation, but it is the love of God that comes near and becomes tangible. When God comes down to our level that we may see him, we can know for certain God's love for us and also how to love one another: the two are joined together. And thus, "God so loved the world, that he gave his only Son" (Jn 3:16) but also, "A new commandment I give to you, that you love one another: just as I have loved you, you also are to love one another" (Jn 13:34). To become a human being, after all, seems like a rather bad idea so far as God is concerned. There is nothing we have that he lacks, and there is much suffering, hardship, and humiliation in this life—in all of which Christ had a full share. But in no other way could God's love be so powerfully communicated than in his willingness to become poor and weak like one of us. It gives us hope in God and hope in our own humanity.

Christ thus renews the image of God in us. He re-heads our race as the new Adam, he reforms our nature and teaches us by our senses, and therefore he also restores our knowledge of God so that we may love him fully as he first loved us. But finally, what it means to be made in God's image (as we have learned previously) is to be capable of sharing in the life that the Trinity has, and this is also the final end of the Incarnation. To sum up this effect of the union of the human and divine in Christ, Athanasius wrote: "He [Christ] indeed assumed humanity that we might become God."[3] Athanasius does not mean by this that we become the transcendent principle that governs the universe, or that we can take a chunk of the divine

---

3 Athanasius, *On the Incarnation* 54.

nature for ourselves, but that we can undergo the process of deification—of becoming truly Godlike. Then "we shall be like him, because we shall see him as he is" (1 Jn 3:2), that is, we will know God truly and therefore become the image we were made to be. Because Christ was God and became man, uniting himself to us in our nature, when we in turn unite ourselves to Christ, we too can have a share in the divine life—and this transformation is only possible when we understand Christ as he is described by the definition of Chalcedon, as one who is fully God and fully man.

14

Why God Suffered and Died

If the Incarnation—the event of Jesus's conception—has renewed our nature, and if we have been given a perfect model of holiness by the life and work of Christ, then why did he have to die on the cross? What remains undone, and why would God have to become man in order to do it? If we recall the divine dilemma that Athanasius proposed, we can see what remains at once. It is not only the damaging of our nature that occurred at the Fall, but also the stated penalty of that damage: death. In order for the way to heaven to be opened for us once again, and in order that the debt of Adam and Eve might be remitted, humankind still owes death. But our death would mean that our nature, even with the possibility of renewal opened by the Incarnation, would perish and that God would lose us whom he loves. We would be restored but not redeemed. Death, therefore, must be conquered, and the Incarnation is the most fitting way for sin and its consequences to be overcome. To connect this idea with the last chapter: Christ had to be fully man and fully God to renew his image in us, but also to save us from death in the way that he did.

One of the classic Christian understandings of why Christ had to suffer and die, and why he had to be fully God and fully man in order to redeem us, comes from St. Anselm's *Cur Deus Homo* (in English, *Why God Became Man*). Anselm's reasoning is as follows: By sinning against the God who made us, to whom we owe our whole existence, we incur a debt that is something like infinity plus one (because God has given us everything, and even then we turned away). Such a debt no creature could pay, since we do not have anything of infinite value or merit. Only God could pay such a tab. However, the debt is not owed by God, but by humankind. Thus, one who is fully God and fully man, Jesus Christ, is able to offer something infinitely valuable (the precious life of the Son of God), and truly to offer it in our place, since he himself is a man. The idea of Christ ransoming us, or paying our price, is found in a number of places in the New Testament. For example: "[Y]ou were ransomed from the futile ways inherited from your forefathers, not with perishable things such as silver or gold, but with the precious blood of Christ, like that of a lamb without blemish or spot" (1 Pt 1:18–19). By comparing Christ's death to money (silver and gold), the image of paying a debt is particularly vivid in 1 Peter. Christ's death pays the debt of sin incurred by us and by our ancestors, with a currency that far exceeds that of worldly wealth. Or, to put it succinctly as Paul does to the Corinthians, "[Y]ou were bought with a price" (1 Cor 6:20; 1 Cor 7:23).

Anselm's answer to the question of the necessity of the cross is easy to understand, and certainly captures the essence of a truth about the redemption that the death of Christ offers, but we have to go deeper if we want to understand how Christ can be said to pay a debt. Indeed, how can we understand a "debt" that is owed to God? God cannot lack anything. By giving us life, he himself is not diminished, and so he is not a creditor in the same way that a human lender would be. God cannot be owed anything such that he would be deficient without payment in full. There is nothing missing from the divine bank account due to our sin. In other words, God would remain whole and entire even if Christ had never died. Moreover, God can appear overly transactional or exacting if we think of him as a heavenly accountant, demanding a payment that he knows we cannot make. Rather the "debt" owed to God is something that works only as an analogy (which, as we know, is how all of our language about God functions). To God we owe everything because from him we receive existence, and when we do not fully give ourselves over to him, we cannot have the fullness of life; there is a lack. That is why sin is death, as we discussed earlier, because when we depart from Life itself, we die. The debt owed to God is one of gratitude, which adds nothing to God, but gives us our proper orientation, because we are created, dependent beings, and we would be living a lie to pretend otherwise. Christ's perfect sacrifice does pay off this debt because he offers to God the complete love and obedience that we refused him, and of which we are incapable without his sacrifice. Christ's death is therefore the completion of all sacrifices offered in the Old Testament. Those sacrifices were training us to cling to God, to give ourselves over, and not to rely on our own strength and material wealth. But we could never sacrifice as fully as Christ did. Why? As one who is God, Christ can give himself without remainder and without owing anything. But, as a human being, he could offer this sacrifice on our behalf, giving to God the gratitude that should define human life. Christ offers this sacrifice, but without the stain of sin, the sin that inhibits us from giving ourselves as a pure and unreserved gift.

It is therefore by uniting our death to the death of Christ that we can rise again. We now have a perfect sacrifice to which we can join ourselves. Paul explains this dynamic of dying with Christ in order to live again in his letter to the Romans:

> We were buried therefore with him by baptism into death, in order that, just as Christ was raised from the dead by the glory of the Father, we too might walk in newness of life. For if we have been united with him in a death like his, we shall certainly be united with him in a resurrection like his. We know that our old self was crucified with him in order that the body of sin might be

brought to nothing, so that we would no longer be enslaved to sin. For one who has died has been set free from sin. (Rom 6:4–7)

We see from Paul that Christ died in our stead not in the sense that he died *instead of us* but that he died *for us* so that we too can die in him in hopes of the resurrection, and that we can make headway against sin in this life as the result of our baptism. If we take Anselm's analogy too far, after all, there would be no reason for us to die at all, because Christ would have "paid the debt," so to speak, and left nothing left for us to contribute. But Christ has paid our debt in an even deeper way, by giving us back the capacity for gratitude. Christ defeated death not by erasing it, but by making it the means to access eternal life. For this reason, the words of the liturgy of John Chrysostom (used in Catholic Byzantine and Eastern Orthodox liturgies) sing of Christ trampling down death by death. Christ defeats death by overcoming death, not by ignoring death, and not by negating human experience and suffering.

There are many other ways beyond the idea of debt to come to an understanding of why the full humanity and divinity of Christ answers the second half of Athanasius's dilemma: the destruction of death. One such way is by understanding the cross as the defeat of the devil. By sinning and yielding to the temptation of the devil, Adam and Eve in some sense gave themselves willingly over into the devil's power. They sold themselves into slavery, and we are all born slaves from our first parents rather than as free people. As the author of Hebrews explains,

Since, therefore the children share in flesh and blood, he [Christ] himself likewise partook of the same things, that through death he might destroy the one who has the power of death, that is, the devil, and deliver all those who through fear of death were subject to lifelong slavery. (Heb 2:14–15)

Christ therefore came as one who is a member of the race of slaves (a human being), but was also one over whom the devil had no legitimate claim (since he is God, without sin). Therefore, when the devil laid claim to Christ on the cross through death, which is the penalty of sin, he lost his previously legitimate claim over the human race, and we were liberated from bondage. We must again, of course, see this power of the devil as only analogous to slavery. God is in control of all things and does not need to fight with the devil as with an equal opponent. Nevertheless, through this imagery of slavery and liberation, God's power is once again shown not to be the kind of power that requires force to achieve its ends. God liberated us by the very means that would have destroyed us—death—and thereby respected the agency of creatures both human and angelic (i.e., the devil). In a memorable image, St. Gregory of Nyssa speaks of Christ as ensnaring the devil like a fisherman: Christ's humanity was the worm that the devil swallowed, not realizing that within that humanity lay the hook (the divinity) upon which he would be caught and defeated,

> hence it was that God, in order to make himself easily accessible to the one who sought a ransom for us [the Devil], veiled himself in our nature. In that way, as it is with a greedy fish, he might swallow the Godhead like a fishhook along with the flesh, which was the bait. Thus, when the life came to dwell with death and light shone upon darkness, the contraries might vanish away.[1]

And so with the imagery of the defeat of the devil, we come upon another way of understanding why Christ was fully God and fully man.

---

1   Gregory of Nyssa, *Catechetical Oration*, trans. Cyril Richardson and Edward Hardy (Philadelphia: Westminster, 1954), 60–62.

The cross, however, should not be separated from the Incarnation, as if salvation were a two-step program (step 1: Jesus's birth and step 2: Jesus's death). Jesus's act of recapitulation, his re-heading and renewing of the human race discussed in the previous chapter, is not a work of the birth of Christ alone, but of his whole life, reaching its completion on the cross. If Christ is the new Adam, the one from whom we can take our renewed humanity, Christ must reverse or re-write the entire story of Adam. The crucial part of that story is undoing the death that Adam brought upon us in the garden. Adam was disobedient unto death—he transgressed the law of God, knowing the penalty. Christ was Adam-in-reverse, he was obedient unto death—he followed the will of God, knowing the cost. Where Adam was proud, Christ was humble, coming down to earth to live a lowly life, which culminated in a humiliating death. As many of the Fathers like to point out, Christ's cross became the new tree of life, recovering the one that Adam forsook, and Christ died on a tree to save us from the death incurred by a tree. It is this kind of reversal to which the book of Revelation refers when it speaks of "the tree of life with its twelve kinds of fruit, yielding its fruit each month. The leaves of the tree were for the healing of the nations" (Rev 22:2). From Christ's side on the cross flows the Church, symbolized by the twelve tribes of Israel and the twelve disciples. Honorius of Autun, summing up the tradition of the cross as recapitulation, writes that "the Tree of Life is the holy cross, whose fruit is the body of Christ, a body such that anyone who eats of it worthily shall not die the death of the soul forever."[2]

More generally speaking, Christ's renewal of our human nature, his recapitulation of our race, would in some sense

---

2   Honorius of Autun, *Expositio 2*, trans. Richard A. Norris Jr., in *The Church's Bible* (Grand Rapids, Mich.: Eerdmans, 2003), 185.

be lacking if he pulled back from death. If Christ was going to take on the entire human condition and restore it, to stop short of taking on this last thing would be to stop short of true solidarity with us sinners. Paul puts it starkly: "For our sake he made him to be sin who knew no sin, so that in him we might become the righteousness of God" (2 Cor 5:21). Although Christ himself did not commit a sin, he truly became a human being and suffered the penalty of sin. It is in this way that human beings can once again be made right before God (or "become the righteousness of God" as Paul says), because Christ recapitulates what it means to be human right down to the bitter end. Christ reclaimed the whole of human life, including death, which he used to manifest his Resurrection.

In a similar way, one could also think of Christ taking on our plight, including death, as a way of applying a cure to every part of our sickness. Unless the divine remedy penetrated into the very depths of our wound, into the wound of mortality by which we are separated from God, we could not be fully healed in order to enter into the divine life. And, like many earthly remedies even now, often the application of medicine or the undergoing of surgery is painful and difficult; it requires endurance to bring about greater healing. Echoing the book of Isaiah, 1 Peter expounds on this theme (that Christ's suffering is a cure): "He himself bore our sins in his body on the tree, that we might die to sin and live to righteousness. By his wounds you have been healed" (1 Pt 2:24). But we might also think of the many outward signs of healing Christ performed on earth as revealing to us his mission of healing our nature entirely. Christ made the lame walk and the blind see. He also healed many lepers, who were considered to be in a state of waking death, since their flesh disintegrated on their body while they were still alive. Christ healing lepers, therefore, was a powerful foreshadowing of his overcoming of death itself. All of these healings, in other words, were not merely displays of Christ's divine power, but they were also signs (as the Gospel of John often calls them). Signs are meant to indicate something beyond themselves, and Jesus's works of healing point in a profound way to the great work of healing he would perform on the cross, when the salve of Life itself would be applied to the sickness of death. St. Augustine is particularly fond of the image of Christ as the great doctor (*Christus medicus*, as Augustine calls him):

> God was crucified, it's all so incredible. Because your disease became so grave that it needed unbelievable remedies to cure it. And indeed that humble doctor came, and found the patient lying sick, he shared his infirmity with him, summoning him to share in his own divinity; he became in his passion a slayer of passions, and dying he was hung on a tree in order to put death to death. He made a food for us, which we were to take, and be cured.[3]

Augustine explains that humility is the cure of pride, and he gives a name to the medicine that Christ's death provided: the Eucharist, which has often been called "the food of immortality," the cure for death. But we can again see how this healing process is perfect and complete because Christ is God (Life itself) and yet he is man, and so the perfect medicine is applied to exactly the right place.

But finally, we must understand that God was in no way bound by necessity to become man and to die in order to save us. In fact, knowing that God was not fastened to the cross by any external law of justice helps us to see clearly the principal reason for the Incarnation and the crucifixion: love. If one cause of the Incarnation was to reveal God's tender care for us, as

---

3   Augustine, *Sermons*, trans. Edmund Hill, vol. 10 (Hyde Park, N.Y.: New City Press, 1995), 341a.1.

discussed at the end of the previous chapter, the cross is the ultimate disclosure of that love. The cross is the full revelation of God as love, because it was out of love (and not strict necessity) that God became man and died rather than saving us in some other way. Here we can pause to remember that in the creed we profess that Christ "suffered under Pontius Pilate, was crucified, died and was buried." In other words, God did not just die, he also suffered. He did not pass away peacefully in his sleep. By taking on a shameful death, a death chosen for him by his very own people, God shows us the depths of his love and what he was willing to endure for our sake. What is at stake in understanding Christ as fully God and fully man is finally, therefore, the understanding of God's character, of his Trinitarian life. When we look·at the crucifix, we can see with our own eyes that God is an eternal exchange of love into which we are invited. If God had not come himself, if he had simply sent someone else to save us, he still could have accomplished his goal. But we would not have the intimate encounter with the Lord that we have in Christ. We would not know God's love firsthand. Chalcedon therefore tells us that God *himself* came, and, as we know from human experience, when someone comes to our aid personally—not by a messenger or delegate—we see their love and we respond to it. Chalcedon also tells us that God came to us as a *human being*. He did not come to us as an illusion, in a costume, or under a pretense. And this one who is both God and man did not draw back from us when faced with death but gave himself up for us. He came to our aid because he himself is our aid. To return to the concept of the communication of idioms, we can see why it is of utmost importance that we can say that "God was born" and "God died."

The two chief effects of the Incarnation according to Athanasius—the restoration of our image and the defeat of death—are summed up by 2 Peter:

His divine power has granted to us all things that pertain to life and godliness, through the knowledge of him who called us to his own glory and excellence, by which he has granted to us his precious and very great promises, so that through them you may become partakers of the divine nature, having escaped from the corruption that is in the world because of sinful desire. (2 Pt 1:3–4)

Here we can see woven together the root of many of the theological reflections of Athanasius. By knowledge of God, given to us by Christ, we are called to share in God's glory. Through Christ we have received the promise of becoming partakers of the divine nature, because we have escaped corruption. These two are the pillars on which we have built our reflection on the full humanity and divinity of Christ: he has allowed us to become participants in the divine life through his Incarnation and by his defeat of sin and death on the cross.

At last, we can see the depths of the beauty of the seemingly abstract theological statement that Christ is one person with two natures. What this definition means is that one who is fully man and fully God came among us, renewed us, died for us, healed us, and showed his love forth in the fullest way conceivable. God could have saved us in some other way instead of becoming man, but that he saved us in this way is a most fitting, perfect, and wonderful way! God's power and love is shown forth because he saves creation through creation, in and by means of the mess that we have made of things—and so we can say with confidence the words of the Exultet: "O happy fault, which won for us so great a savior!"

15

God in Heaven

Because God became man, man might become like God. Because God died on the cross, we now die but rise again. To what end does this redemption won by Christ bring us? The answer is heaven. But heaven in the modern world is often undersold. To some people, heaven has even come to seem rather boring, because they imagine heaven as a small group of holy people singing pious hymns, picturing some eternal version of the worst church service they have ever attended. And although it is true that in heaven there will be unceasing worship of God, such a notion has become so bland that in popular culture hell is sometimes portrayed as being a lot more fun than heaven. Indeed, there are people who will choose hell over heaven, but this choice will hopefully not be based on a faulty understanding of what heaven really is. Only slightly better are those who see heaven as the sum total of all the things they enjoy on earth. To these people, heaven is reduced to a kind of eternal wish fulfillment, where they can eat candy forever without feeling sick and go surfing from morning until evening. But heaven is not boring, nor is it a room full of all the best things on the earth. Heaven is the vision of God (often called "the beatific vision," which means the happy or blessed vision). As Paul so eloquently puts it: "now we see in a mirror dimly, but then face to face. Now I know in part; then I shall know fully, even as I have been fully known" (1 Cor 13:12).

At the beginning of this book, we set out to seek God in order to know him more, and to recognize that God reveals himself because he wishes to be known and loved. In the end, in heaven, we will fully attain this desire—to know God and to be known by him, to love God, and to fully experience his love.

It is difficult to imagine or to put into words what this experience will then be like, and therefore perhaps it can be hard to whet the appetite of those who think that heaven is no fun or that heaven is an endless chocolate bar. Paul is especially reticent to describe it, writing "What no eye has seen, nor ear heard, nor the heart of man imagined, what God has prepared for those who love him" (1 Cor 2:9). We must therefore know that heaven exceeds whatever happiness we can try to imagine. Frank Sheed compares our attempts to grasp the joys of heaven to a child's attempt to grasp the joy of poetry, in the face of being told poetry is far superior to the joy of playing with a tin soldier.[1] We, like the child, are tempted to think that the joys we have are pretty good and that we would rather hold on to them (and even multiply them). But when we have grown up we no longer have an appetite for tin soldiers. St. John Henry Newman reflects on how inadequate a heaven full of earthly pleasures would be, writing:

> I know . . . from sad experience I am too sure that whatever is created, whatever is earthly, pleases but for a time and then palls and is a weariness. I believe that there is nothing at all here below that I would not at length get sick of. I believe, that though I had all the means of happiness that this life could give, yet in time I would tire of living, feeling everything trite and dull and unprofitable.[2]

---

1   Frank Sheed, *Theology and Sanity* (San Francisco: Ignatius Press, 1993), 344.

2   John Henry Newman, *Everyday Meditations* (Manchester, N.H.: Sophia Institute Press, 2013), 164.

Newman puts before us the true horror of an everlasting life that is nothing more than the goods we can obtain in this life. In our life on earth, we do experience true joy that can be for us a foretaste of heavenly bliss, but the joys of this life are not eternal joys. We know more and more from the experience of growing older that none of these earthly things could fulfill us forever. As Paul says, "When I was a child, I spoke like a child, I thought like a child, I reasoned like a child. When I became a man, I gave up childish ways" (1 Cor 13:11). It is this maturation that, for him, will end in the vision of God and the full attainment of love. It is this joy alone that will satisfy us when we have grown to maturity in Christ. As Newman also concludes: "you, O my God, are ever new, though you are the most ancient—you alone are the food for eternity... you alone are inexhaustible, and ever offer to me something new to know, something new to love."[3] We do know a few things about what heaven will be like, however, even if our imagination fails to picture it. These things about heaven follow logically from what we know about who God is and how he has acted in history. First, we know that in heaven we will be most fully ourselves, which, after the final resurrection, includes our bodies. Of the bodily resurrection, Paul writes that it will happen "in a moment, in the twinkling of an eye, at the last trumpet. For the trumpet will sound, and the dead will be raised imperishable, and we shall be changed" (1 Cor 15:52). Paul compares our earthly bodies to our heavenly by using the analogy of a seed. Just as a seed truly *is* the plant that comes from the seed, so our earthly bodies are the same bodies as the heavenly, and yet they will be transformed (cf. 1 Cor 15:37–38). This doctrine is one that should give to us the greatest comfort with regard to the afterlife, because what it means is that we will not be absorbed into a heavenly ocean,

---

3   Ibid., 165.

nor will we be a kind of placid angel strumming a harp, but we will continue to be truly ourselves. If God created us to be free participants in his love, it makes sense for us to retain that freedom forever. And, if the Incarnation gives us hope of being human and reaffirms the dignity of the human race, we should be encouraged even more by the resurrection of the body, knowing that this restoration of dignity is not temporary but permanent. As we know, we image God by our intellects, but also by our whole person because of our soul-body unity. Therefore, we can know that this image of God that we bear will be perfected and eternal in heaven.

But many people today, even Christians, speak of the body as if it were only a shell and seem to believe that our final redemption will be an escape from our body. But the true Christian hope is much greater. Just as Christ defeated death by taking on death, he redeems the body through the body. God's creation that was made good in the beginning will show forth that goodness forever in heaven. The problems we experience with the body now because of illness, hunger, and the like exist because our souls are not fully in tune with our bodies, and because our bodies are mortal. When we are raised incorruptible, we will not put aside the bodies in which we have lived our whole lives on earth, but we will have them finally as we were meant to have them. The doctrine of the resurrection of the body is in perfect harmony with the doctrine of creation, because God made us who we are, soul and body, and made us for love of him; we will most fully be who we were created to be in heaven. In this life we often feel misunderstood. We struggle for balance and for health. We make resolutions but cannot keep them. We act in ways that we wish we did not. How many popular songs, after all, lament things like the complexity of love, the regret of missed opportunity, or the pain of being rejected and deceived? How many works of literature express frustration at being misrepresented or our inability to express ourselves and to be understood? The promise, therefore, of being completely integrated, known, and accepted, completely healthy and holy, should be welcome indeed. For this reason, our Lord tells us that "whoever would save his life will lose it, but whoever loses his life for my sake will find it" (Mt 16:25). What we find in heaven is our true life, our true selves, and we lose the imperfections, false starts, and inordinate attachments that so plague our life on earth. We give ourselves over to Christ, and in return we receive his renewed life as our own.

Secondly, we know that communion with God and with each other is the sum of the promise of heaven. The images that Jesus often uses in his teaching help us to envision this. He describes heaven in many places as a feast, one where "many will come from east and west and recline at table with Abraham, Isaac, and Jacob in the kingdom of heaven" (Mt 8:11). Our forefathers in faith awaiting us at the table is for us an image of the joyful reunion of all those who have died in the peace of Christ. Sharing a banquet is a relatable concept that represents—both for us and for the ancients—being in happy fellowship. More specifically, heaven is envisioned as a wedding feast, with people gathered from all around so that the wedding hall is packed with guests (e.g., Mt 22:1–14). The image of us joining God in his wedding feast is the culmination of the love story told throughout the Scriptures, which, as we have seen already, is often described using bridal imagery (e.g., in the Song of Songs).

The image of marriage is also seen in the book of Revelation, in John's ecstatic vision of heavenly worship,

> Then I heard what seemed to be the voice of a great multitude, like the roar of many waters and like the sound of mighty peals of thunder, crying out,
> "Hallelujah!
> For the Lord our God

the Almighty reigns.
Let us rejoice and exult ·
    and give him the glory,
for the marriage of the Lamb has come,
    and his Bride has made herself ready;
it was granted her to clothe herself
    with fine linen, bright and pure"—
for the fine linen is the righteous deeds of the saints.

And the angel said to me, "Write this: Blessed are those who are invited to the marriage supper of the Lamb." And he said to me, "These are the true words of God." (Rev 19:6–9)

In the image of the wedding feast found in the book of Revelation, we return to the vision of heaven as the endless worship of God, because the wedding feast of the Lamb is not just a happy occasion for human fellowship; it is the marriage of the human (the Church) to the divine. Here the Church is clothed in the deeds of the saints, having washed herself clean in the blood of the Lamb (cf. Rev 7:14), ready to give herself wholly over to Christ whom she loves. And what is worship of God other than this? Other than full entrustment in love and gratitude, exulting, rejoicing, and praising with heart and mind? So, the marriage feast of the Lamb, which is heaven, is the worship of God by his saints. It is our own marriage feast, the perfect communion of heaven and earth. Knowing the doctrine of the Trinity, what else should we expect to find in heaven other than God himself who is a perfect communion of love? This Trinitarian life of perfect unity-in-diversity is the life that we will embrace fully when at last we see God, when we know him and love him. Pope Benedict XVI, preaching on the feast of the assumption of the Virgin, describes heaven in this way:

Today's feast impels us to lift our gaze to Heaven; not to a heaven consisting of abstract ideas or even an imaginary heaven created by art, but the Heaven of true reality which is God himself. God is Heaven. He is our destination, the destination and the eternal dwelling place from which we come and for which we are striving.[4]

Theologians and authors of all stripes have tried their hand at describing heaven in a way that is appealing and by which we might have some small foretaste of its goodness. Augustine, for example, reflects on it many places, but perhaps at greatest length in his book *The City of God*, which traces the whole narrative of salvation history from its beginning amongst the angels all the way to the final judgment and resurrection. He wrestles with the question of whether or not we will be able to see God somehow with bodily eyes (since we will have our bodies again), and he offers this reflection on the beatific vision:

> God will be so known by us and will be so much before us, that we will see him by the spirit in ourselves, in one another, in himself, in the new heavens and the new earth, in every created thing which will then exist; and also by the body we will see him in every body which the keen vision of the eye of the spiritual body will reach.[5]

The harmony that Augustine proposes here unites the insights gained from the Gospels (such as feasting at a common table) and that of Revelation (where the saints fall down to worship before the awesome sight of God). The vision of God does not mean that we will be seized in a kind of ecstatic trance, where we look at God without being who we are or without thought of anything else. Rather, God will be "so much before us," as Augustine says, that wherever we look and whatever we do, we

---

4   Benedict XVI, Homily on the Solemnity of the Assumption of the Blessed Virgin Mary (St. Thomas of Villanova Parish, Castel Gandolfo, August 15, 2008).

5   Augustine, *City of God*, trans. Marcus Dods (New York: Random House, 2000), 22.29.

will be seeing God, because our vision will be enabled by God. The vision of other people will be for us the vision of God. The vision of the new heavens and the new earth will be for us the vision of God. In everything, we will see and experience the love of God, and so finally the two great commandments—to love God and to love our neighbor—will be fulfilled in complete harmony. Augustine also summarizes our hope of the hereafter as the perfection of the image of the Trinity in us: "There our being will have no death, our knowledge no error, our love no mishap."[6] If we recall Augustine's image of the Trinity (memory, understanding, and will), we will see him using that image here as well, in putting forth the idea that what makes us in the image of the Trinity will be secure and perfected in heaven. We will exist with no fear of forgetting or being forgotten; we will understand all and love rightly.

In the Latin funeral Mass (also called the *requiem* Mass), images of rest and light predominate. The entrance antiphon, which is still used in the modern funeral Mass, is "Eternal rest grant them, O Lord, and perpetual light shine on them." These themes are echoed again and again throughout the liturgy: in the offertory ("let the holy stand-bearer Michael show them into that holy light which long ago you promised to Abraham and his seed"), in the *Agnus Dei* (where "have mercy on us" is replaced by "grant them eternal rest"), and in the *Lux Aeterna*, sometimes used now as the Communion antiphon ("May light eternal shine upon them, Lord, with your saints in eternity: since you are merciful. Eternal rest grant to them, Lord, and let perpetual light shine upon them: with your saints in eternity, since you are merciful"). These images of light and rest echo not so much what Jesus says about his kingdom, but what he says about himself, since heaven is our full communion with Christ, and through him the Trinity.

---

6   Ibid., 11.28.

Christ tells us, "I am the light of the world. Whoever follows me will not walk in darkness, but will have the light of life" (Jn 8:12). The Gospel of John has plenty of images of Christ as the light, for example, right near the very beginning of the Gospel: "In him was life, and the life was the light of men. The light shines in the darkness, and the darkness has not overcome it" (Jn 1:4). Of his own rest, Christ says: "Come to me, all who labor and are heavy laden, and I will give you rest. Take my yoke upon you, and learn from me, for I am gentle and lowly in heart, and you will find rest for your souls. For my yoke is easy, and my burden is light" (Mt 11:28–30). And Paul tells us that "he himself is our peace" (Eph 2:14). In all of these words, we are told that in Christ himself we will find our heaven, he who is our light and our rest.

Light imagery, in particular, is also highly complementary to the idea of heaven as perfect vision that we have been discussing. It is by light that we can see and, in heaven, the light by which we see will be God himself. St. Gregory of Nazianzus (also called Gregory the Theologian) is particularly fond of citing Psalm 36 to make this point: "For with you is the fountain of life; in your light do we see light" (Ps 36:9). Gregory understands this verse to mean that God *is* the light by which we will see him. Dante in his *Paradiso* also favors images of light in order to spark our imagination about the heavenly life. In the final canto of his poem, when Dante finally beholds the light of the Trinity in the highest realm of heaven, he describes it both as vision and healing of vision:

> O overbrimming grace whence I presumed
>   to gaze upon the everlasting Light
>   so fully that my vision consumed!
> I saw the scattered elements unite,
>   bound all with love into one book of praise
>   in the deep ocean of the infinite

Substance and accident and all their ways
    as if breathed into one: and understand,
      my words are a weak glimmer in the haze.[7]

Dante's poem is actually quite similar to Augustine's more theological explanation of the vision we will have in heaven. In gazing on the everlasting light that is God, we will experience perfect unity of all "scattered elements." We will be enabled to see by the one who is our sight. In other words, the harmony between all things that we strive for in this life will be obtained, and this harmony is achieved by love and is bound in one "book of praise." Worship of God is not a servile or boring activity, but the expression of love by all things held together in that eternal light. Our vision will be fully consumed by God, as Dante's, and yet we will see all. Here Dante tries to express in his own words—however imperfectly, as he admits—what Paul also says of the final consummation of the ages: God will be all in all (cf. 1 Cor 15:28).

---

7   Dante, *Paradise,* trans. Anthony Esolen (New York: Random House, 2007), 33.82–90.

DO YOU KNOW
WHAT EVERY CATHOLIC
SHOULD KNOW?

The new What Every Catholic Should Know book series is written for everyday Catholics looking to explore the beauty and culture of our faith. Each author in the series takes a panoramic view of a unique topic and presents it in an approachable, easy-to-read format. Published by the trusted theologians of the Augustine Institute, the What Every Catholic Should Know book series will help any Catholic go deeper in their faith.

LEARN MORE AT **EveryCatholic.org**